U N E X P E C T E D   G R A C E

uNexpecteD
gRace

Preaching Good News from Difficult Texts

GENNIFER BENJAMIN BROOKS

THE PILGRIM PRESS

CLEVELAND

tHis BOOK is dedicated to
Patsy and Lorna (Pearl and Akua) in
celebration of our girlhood together.

The Pilgrim Press, 700 Prospect Avenue, Cleveland, Ohio 44115
thepilgrimpress.com
© 2012 by Gennifer Benjamin Brooks

Scripture quotations, unless otherwise noted, are from the New Revised
Standard Version of the Bible, © 1989 by the Division of Christian Education
of the National Council of Churches of Christ in the United States of America,
and are used by permission. Changes have been made for inclusivity.

Printed in the United States of America on acid-free paper

16   15   5   4   3   2

Library of Congress Cataloging-in-Publication Data

Brooks, Gennifer Benjamin, 1947–
    Unexpected grace : preaching good news from difficult texts /
Gennifer Benjamin Brooks.
        p. cm.
    Includes bibliographical references.
    ISBN 978-0-8298-1938-0 (alk. paper)
    1. Bible—Homiletical use.   I. Title.
BS534.5.B76 2012
    251—dc23   2012008799

CONTENTS

vii   PREFACE

1   **1**   NAMING TROUBLE

17   **2**   A TROUBLESOME GOD

43   **3**   IN THE FAMILY OF GOD

70   **4**   FOR THE SAKE OF THE COMMUNITY

95   **5**   LIVING A HOLY LIFE

124   **6**   SAVING GRACE

133   APPENDIX A: *Methodology for Developing Good News Sermons from Difficult Texts*

135   APPENDIX B: *Guidelines for Analysis of the Context*

137   APPENDIX C: *Guidelines for Homiletical Exegesis for Good News Preaching*

139   APPENDIX D: *Guidelines for Developing the Good News Statement and the Message Statement*

140   NOTES

145   BIBLIOGRAPHY

PREFACE

•   •   •

ONe of the great accomplishments of my childhood was reading the Bible from cover to cover. It was a moment of great triumph, and the fact that so much in the Bible was difficult to understand did not matter. It was a major milestone for a preteenage child who was growing up in the church. Of course, most of what I read did not stick and I ignored the difficult passages that did not make sense to my biblically and theologically unsophisticated mind. As I have listened to many preachers over the years, I have too often had the unfortunate sense that my childhood experience is the same for many preachers. It is not that I believe that they have read the Bible from cover to cover as I did—in fact, I become more convinced each day that many preachers have not ever read the Bible in its entirety—but I am convinced that in too many cases they simply pass over any part of the biblical text that they consider problematic. My conclusion is based on the fact that so many preachers are unable to articulate fully the good news of God's covenantal, transformative love that runs through the entire biblical record.

Offering good news in every sermon is an important issue for me. I believe that the substance of divine grace as a mitigating factor against human weakness and sin is the critical element of every sermon. The written evidence of that good news, and thus the foundation of every sermon, is found in the entire canon of scripture. Therefore, as important for me as good news preaching is the issue of unread and unpreached texts. My concern is that not only have many preachers neglected the reading of some texts that may be critical to a better understanding of the divine/human relationship, but also some texts that they have read have been misinterpreted and mispreached because of the difficulty these passages of scripture represent in interpreting them for preaching in particular contexts.

Having addressed the issue of preaching good news in every sermon in *Good News Preaching*,[1] I based the impetus for this book on two factors. First was the realization that while every sermon needs to offer transformative good news,[2] not every biblical text presents apparent or easily deciphered good news for preaching. On the whole, many, if not most, preachers avoid addressing recognizably difficult texts of scripture. Even where the lectionary is the basis for selection, not only does it sanitize texts that seem challenging for preaching, but preachers also generally stick to those texts that they consider can be easily interpreted or applied to their hearers. On the other hand, in cases where the preacher accepts the challenge of addressing difficult texts, there is often a surface reading of the words of scripture applied in such a facile manner that the real meaning or use of the text is missed or misapplied, or there may be such detailed interpretation offered in the sermon that it becomes a lecture about the text rather than a sermon that offers a gospel message.

My second driver, which inspired the juxtaposition of trouble and grace, arose from my study of the four-page style of sermon structure developed by Paul Scott Wilson.[3] Although I greatly appreciate and use Wilson's work, I came to realize that while the idea of trouble and grace exemplifying the divine/human relationship is readily apparent in many biblical passages, there are many other passages of scripture that challenge the facile use of the model. Cases where only trouble seems apparent and passages where the free grace of God denies any aspect of human responsibility require the preacher to do extensive analysis of both the biblical text and the preaching context in order to bring the text to life for the context of the sermon. This is even more critical in the present postmodern culture, which balks at the idea of absolute truth and which subjects both the nature of God and humanity and the understanding of divine sovereignty and human fallibility to uncritical analysis and unsubstantiated conclusions.

Since I am committed to the idea of all preaching being about offering the transformative good news of the divine/human relationship, there seemed to be a definite call to address the issue of trouble and grace in light of a genre of texts that may qualify as "difficult" for preaching. My interest led to the development of a course that I subsequently taught for two years at the Doctor of Ministry level for the Association of Chicago Theological Schools (ACTS). The first year the course was entitled Preaching Good News from the Whole Bible; the second year, I used a different title that I considered more directly representative of the material—Preaching Good News from Difficult Texts. The students in those two years of classes provided additional inspiration, and their struggles with self-selected difficult texts assisted in convincing me that preachers might be helped by materials and methods that were targeted deliberately and specifically for dealing with Bible texts that require extensive interpretation for preaching good news. The purpose of this book is to help those adventurous or diligent preachers who wish to accept the challenge of preaching good news from the whole Bible, including the difficult texts.

This work will be guided using four specific criteria to categorize the textual difficulty in the divine/human relationships as recorded in the biblical texts. Using selected passages of scripture that represent these categories, following an introductory description of textual difficulties, four chapters will provide homiletical ideas and strategies for analyzing and interpreting the particular type of difficulty that will help preachers find good news for preaching. Although of necessity this book offers limited biblical interpretation of selected texts, it does not represent itself as a Bible commentary. In fact it relies heavily on *The New Interpreter's Bible Commentary* (Nashville: Abingdon Press, 1994–1998),[4] since I believe that the scholarship required for developing Bible commentaries is best left in the hands of Bible scholars. The focus of this work is on homiletical strategies aimed at developing good news sermons from Bible texts that may be difficult to preach because of the texts themselves or the context in which they are to be preached. Borrowing language from Catherine Gunsalus Gonzales, this book is in a very limited but, I hope, helpful way a preaching commentary.[5] To be even more specific based on the substance of this material, it might be considered a "Good News Preaching Commentary."

Chapter 1 provides a foundation for understanding the challenge of preaching past the difficulty in biblical texts in a way that offers genuine good news. It also offers a methodological process for developing good news sermons in the face of textual or contextual difficulties. Chapters 2 through 5 will each deal with a different genre of difficulty. Each chapter incorporates Bible passages that fit the criteria for that genre. For each of the texts addressed there is a brief analysis of possible difficulties of the congregational context and issues of interpretation of the text that may impact the preacher's task of developing a good news sermon. At the end of each chapter there is a sermon that relates to the particular genre of difficulty. Each sermon has been given the same title as that of the chapter in which it appears.

Chapter 2 focuses on the nature of God. It addresses the difficulty of preaching good news when the text seems to reveal a picture of God that is contrary to human expectation or when it seems that God is uncaring, absent, or uninvolved in the lives of God's people. Chapter 3 looks at family systems as they are portrayed in scripture, especially when they seem representative of dysfunction and the trouble and grace they present, sometimes simultaneously. The focus will be on the model of biblical family life that offers support or advises caution for today's families. For example, how does the preacher offer good news from texts that seem to show divine favoritism of one person or family group over another in a way that encourages human sinfulness, evil, or injustice? Chapter 4 turns the spotlight on human nature revealed in the shaping of and life in community. From the beginning of creation, God has been actively engaged in building a community that will offer a picture of the realm of God. To that end, the chapter also explores the issues of justice in community living. It addresses the challenge of preaching good news when both individual and corporate actions of the people of God exemplify injustice, oppression, and violence against the powerless.

Chapter 5 looks at biblical texts whose difficulty arises mainly from their use in particular contexts. The selected texts are concerned with the rules of life and holy living that relate to the laws and directives given to the children of God throughout time. Many of these texts might not generally be considered difficult, but because of the situation of the congregation or the daring of the preacher they may present serious challenges for an offering of good news that can be heard in the application of the text to current issues of life. It also focuses directly on the revelation of grace in the lives of all people and the challenge of free or easy grace as a source of trouble for the recipients. It looks in part at the way in which the favor of God, seen as a right, shapes or misleads the people of God as they strive to live holy lives.

Chapter 6, the concluding chapter, invites preachers into the fray that is the work of preaching good news from difficult texts. The invitation is also a challenge to pastors and other preachers to debunk the notion that some texts are to be ignored because of their intrinsic difficulty. Without any apology, it is in fact a dare to those preachers who have approached certain biblical texts with fear and trepidation only to walk away beaten and bloody after trying to wring an appropriate Christian message from words that seem to have a life of their own, that seem to offer violence, pain, and even death. Above all, it is a call to preachers to delve deeply into the biblical record and through it to witness to their faith in the covenantal love of God present in all of scripture. It reprises the challenges to be faced and the strategies that may be employed to recognize and overcome the difficulty a text presents to the preaching moment in order to preach relevant and appropriate good news. It points to an opportunity for preachers to address the whole Bible—even difficult texts—with the authority and passion of their call and a commitment to offer the gospel in every sermon.

I am grateful to the many seminary students who willingly struggle in my classes to find the good news for preaching in the assigned texts. Every student who successfully takes on the challenge confirms for me that the task of finding good news is worth the effort and that preaching transformative good news is an essential offering of divine love to needy souls. I am grateful as well to the many preachers, both laity and ordained clergy, who express their appreciation for new ways of thinking about preaching and proclaiming good news. Loving and grateful thanks to my prayer partner, Mrs. Iris Green, for typing the manuscript and, most importantly, for being such an integral part of my life.

Heartfelt gratitude to my colleague in ministry, Rev. Preston Price, who took on the challenge of reading and editing the raw manuscript (typing errors and all) and challenged me in significant ways to sharpen the work. Thanks also to my dear friends and colleagues Rev. Leo W. Curry and Rev. Cynthia Belt for their willingness to read and respond to the manuscript, and to my colleagues in the field of homiletics Ron Allen and Gary V. Simpson for their willingness to say a kind word about the work.

Thanks for the friendship and support of my seminary colleagues Dr. Reginald Blount, Dr. Cheryl Anderson, and Dr. Ruth Duck and for the collegiality of the entire faculty of Garrett-Evangelical Theological Seminary. Grateful thanks also to a supportive sisterhood of clergywomen—Rev. Cynthia Wilson, Dr. Pamela Lightsey, Rev. Denise Pickett, Rev. Diane Bogues, Rev. Jacqueline Ford, and Rev. Dr. Ouida Lee—and to my sister-friends, Mrs. Helen Ammons, Ms. Hortence Drew, and Mrs. Cynella Simon. Finally, thanks to all the members of my natural and extended family for their continued love and support.

My hope is that this material will be helpful to clergy and lay preachers alike. It is written in simple language so that its contents can be as available and of assistance to the beginning preacher, the seminary student, and even the practiced preacher who dares to preach good news from the whole Bible.

Above all, thanks to God for every good and perfect gift.

· 1 ·

NAMING TROUBLE

IN *Good News Preaching*, I named three essential requirements for preaching good news in every sermon.[1] The first of these was "a theology of Good News."[2] In order to preach good news from the whole Bible, the preacher must first accept and live into the belief, unswervingly, that the covenantal love of God is present in all of scripture. Whatever effort it takes to unearth it, the good news of the divine/human covenant, the common thread that is woven through law and prophets, history and poetry of the Old Testament, and that finds fulfillment in the New Testament through Jesus Christ, must be made visible to the people of God at every event of preaching. They must see the face of God looking down, the hands of Christ reaching out, and the Spirit of God lifting them up so that the life they live can be a holy life through God's enlivening, transforming, and empowering grace.

We live in a world of sound bites and happy endings to major problems of life that come to fruition in an hour or even in half an hour on television. Worse yet, the preacher has in most cases barely fifteen minutes within a typical worship service to tell the story and offer good news. It is no wonder that so many sermons fall far short of meeting the requirement of presenting transformative good news to the gathered community. That is not to say that longer preaching time automatically means better sermons. It does not. The conscientious preacher can say and do more to offer the assurance of grace and help to strengthen the discipleship of the hearers in a short sermon than those who have given short shrift to the text can do in much lengthier sermons.

The requirement for preaching good news in every sermon is predicated on the belief that the hearers need new and fresh supplies of grace constantly in order to meet the continuing and new challenges of life. The call on the preacher is to confront the troubles that plague the hearers and the world armed with grace that can overcome. This requires that the preacher approach all of scripture with understanding and faith that it contains a word that will speak in some way to the human condition. At times, however, that good word is hidden beneath the debris of situations in the text or cannot be received by the congregation because of situations in the preaching context. The good news may be lost in cloudy representations of divine grace and stark and unrelenting evidence of human sinfulness. It is at times like these that preaching good news is difficult. The texts may be difficult in and of themselves or as they are brought into the context of the sermon.

THE DIFFICULTY

In my reading of scripture, and in particular, reading scripture in preparation for preaching, there are times when the meaning of the text in its context is clouded by unfamiliar language and hidden nuances. Beyond that, there are those texts whose very content seem to make them immediately improper or inappropriate for whole groups of people. Consider the directive "slaves obey your earthly masters with fear and trembling, in singleness of heart, as you obey Christ" (Eph. 6:5) preached to an African American congregation whose historical experience of slavery in the United States continues to be manifest in oppressive structures and hegemonic policies of society. The preacher confronted with this dilemma may choose simply to bypass the text instead of trying to overcome what seems like an insurmountable task of finding good news, or perhaps may overanalyze the text and deliver a lecture based on the analysis instead of the expected sermon. In the same way a preacher may subvert Jesus' message as Luke records it— "Blessed are you who are poor, for yours is the kingdom of God" (Luke 6:20b)—or Matthew's rendition of Jesus' teaching on money—"Do not store up for yourselves treasures on earth. . . . For where your treasure is, there your heart will be also" (Matt. 6:19a, 21)—when faced with a congregation of financially rich people.

In both cases the difficulty of the text lies obviously in the context in which it is to be preached, but there may be other issues of difficulty that are connected to the text itself that makes it challenging for preachers in other contexts. Take, for example, Jesus' Palm Sunday tirade in the temple: "Then Jesus entered the temple and drove out all who were selling and buying in the temple, and he overturned the tables of the money changers and the seats of those who sold doves" (Matt. 21:12). Long before the preacher has adequately explained Jesus' rationale or the source of his anger, someone who is basically biblically illiterate (as a large percentage of churchgoers today are) might begin to wonder about Christ, who speaks so strongly against anger while demonstrating such anger and violence. And perhaps a child, or young person, or even an adult, hearing the text might use it as justification for their inappropriate or abusive behavior.

These simple examples are hardly even the tip of the homiletical iceberg as one approaches the issue of preaching good news from difficult texts. In fact, some may rightly make the case that there are challenges to be overcome in the preaching of all texts and in offering good news in every sermon. I believe it is an incontrovertible truth that, in the divine/human relationship, the good news is always divine grace that is offered freely to sinful humanity as the enabling force for righteous living as Christians. Difficultly arises when the divine relationship seems to offer anything but grace and when the sinfulness of humanity—be it oppression, injustice, violence, or any other iterations of sinful human nature—seems an acceptable norm or is approved or even demanded by God, as evidenced in this text:

> *Then the Lord said to Moses, "Stretch out your hand over the sea,*
> *so that the water may come back upon the Egyptians, upon their*

chariots and chariot drivers." So Moses stretched out his hand over the sea, and at dawn the sea returned to its normal depth. As the Egyptians fled before it, the Lord tossed the Egyptians into the sea. The waters returned and covered the chariots and the chariot drivers, the entire army of Pharaoh that had followed them into the sea; not one of them remained. (Exod. 14:26–28)

This seems like a clear case of favoritism, bias, or even prejudice that shows preference to the Hebrews and an absence of God's grace for the hapless Egyptians. In such cases as these, when applied to the context of the world today where preference of one racial or cultural group over another has caused the favored group to try to annihilate the other, the texts themselves become difficult.

Gonzalez posits that "when we speak of difficult or challenging passages of Scripture, the difficulty is intrinsic not necessarily to the passage itself, but to the way in which it confronts us in our own particular situation."[3] The truth of that statement requires no debate, but as she recognizes in further expansion of her proposition, there are times when the texts themselves become difficult because of the prevailing situation in the greater society, the church, or the world; "when specific issues become a dominant subject of controversy in the church and probably also in the wider society, and biblical passages that directly touch the topic become themselves the focus of debate."[4] Particularly in such cases the people of God need the assurance of God's continued grace, and when the biblical text seems to offer the contrary, the task of the preacher takes on herculean proportions as it looms precariously on the insecure balance of biblical interpretation and congregational analysis. Good news preaching compounds the difficulty, as it requires the preacher to "approach the text with prayerful expectation of finding good news."[5] Where text and situation are at cross purposes, they conspire to hide or obliterate the offering of divine grace present in scripture.

TROUBLE AND GRACE

"Preaching is the proclamation of the Gospel to the people of God in a particular time and place."[6] This statement taken from my first textbook on preaching is foundational to my homiletical theology. It represents my unswerving belief that every sermon must be intentional and specific about offering good news. This definition of preaching also takes seriously Paul's word to Timothy on the value and purpose of scripture. "All scripture is inspired by God and is useful for teaching, for reproof, for correction, and for training in righteousness, so that everyone who belongs to God may be proficient, equipped for every good work" (2 Tim. 3:16–17). The Bible offers written witness of God's relationship with humanity and, as the inspired word of God, is foundational to Christian understanding of God's covenantal, redemptive love for humanity.

In the proclamation of the gospel the preacher is given an opportunity to help the people of God experience for themselves an assurance of God's grace operating in their lives for their present and ultimate good. The sermon to be crafted from a particular text or in response to a situation that is particularly troublesome challenges the preacher's interpretive and imaginative capabilities. In its most basic rendition, the message of the sermon that describes the juxtaposition of trouble and grace, which is the substance of the divine/human relationship, may require simple application of the biblical record of God's active presence in the lives of individuals, communities, and nations over time to the present context. It is the premise that undergirds Paul Scott Wilson's four-page method of sermon development.

In his attempt "to encourage preachers to be biblical, grounding their sermons in the biblical text, and allowing the text to 'speak' the sermon,"[7] Wilson proposes that preachers divide the content of their sermons into four distinct pages or theological tasks. The content of the four pages comes from four different kinds of material we can include in our sermons. Basically we are confined to talking about: (1) sin and brokenness in the biblical world, (2) sin and brokenness in our world, (3) grace in the biblical world, and (4) grace in our world.[8]

From my experience in teaching Wilson's method of sermon development and from using the four-page style for several of my own sermons, I have come to appreciate the methodology and to applaud its value in helping preachers to present biblical and theological ideas clearly and also to encourage their homiletical imagination. However, also for these reasons, I have come to recognize that there are texts that do not fall easily into this structure and require greater depth of analysis and extensive application of the creative imagination, which Wilson invites his preachers to use in the sermon process in order to be faithful to the text and to allow the sermon to offer authentic good news that can impact the hearers in constructive ways in their particular context.[9]

The Bible offers both historical and theological bases for the proclamation of the good news of God's grace gifted freely to humanity. It also provides evidence of the influence of sin that is the initiator of human trouble. This insight into the covenantal relationship between God and human beings through which the grace of God is the mediator against the trouble that results from human sinfulness is the exemplar for claiming the presence of God active and available in the present. The preacher is called to interpret the time-honored words in a way that authentically engages the lives of the people to whom the sermon is being preached. Through this process, preaching offers the gathered community an opportunity to experience and celebrate the love of God that enables them to live fully into their identity as the redeemed children of God. When the contents of the text or the meanings attached to the text overshadow that existential Christian truth, good news is hard to find and harder to preach.

There are many circumstances under which Bible texts may be considered "difficult." The following criteria were used in my seminary classes to apply the identifier of "difficult" to a biblical text:

- The nature of God—when the text seems to reveal a divine nature contrary to normal expectation or less than or opposite to that usually associated with God; or that God is deliberately absent and unconcerned with the needs of the people.

- The action of God in the lives of the people—when God seems to have acted in ways that are unjust and offensive or when God's judgment in response to human sinfulness is extreme and severely punishing.

- Human evil—a biblical text that describes human actions that are evil, especially when such action is presented as appropriate human activity in the community and the world.

- High degree of oppression and injustice—where injustice and oppression run unchecked without divine intervention or relief, or seemingly with divine approbation.

- Challenge or condemnation of the status quo—biblical texts that speak directly to present congregational situations, particularly those of oppression and injustice.

By no means are these criteria all-inclusive of the challenges faced by preachers as they encounter difficulty in developing a text for preaching good news. In fact as I began to develop the material for this book, I was confronted by several different situations with biblical texts that were so clearly representative of some in the present society and culture that they demanded attention.

For example, the problem of domestic abuse, incest, and violence are currently on the center stage in the United States and in many nations across the world. Families and family systems gone awry and the challenges and problems of trying to live a holy life in the face of overwhelming temptations and seductive inducements play out in the media daily. There are also issues in the church, ecclesial and ecclesiological, that are being experienced on both individual and corporate levels, and there are biblical texts that seem to hit directly in the center of the issue, to the chagrin of those in the church—both laity and clergy. Thus a text that directly addresses the issue becomes difficult to hear. At other times, congregations are beaten down or unjustifiably applauded by the inappropriate or erroneous use of some biblical texts in preaching. The reality is that a text that may be full of good news for a particular congregation may present great difficulty in its presentation to another congregation or even to the same congregation at a different time. Many preachers are left floundering as they are confronted with the responsibility to offer good news despite the challenges presented by the text or by the congregation's particular context.

GOOD NEWS PREACHING

Preaching good news on every occasion calls for a high level of imagination and interpretation. Wilson encourages preachers to use the tactics employed in movie making in order to engage the text and context imaginatively.[10] It bears repeating that preaching good news from difficult texts requires great imagination and interpretive techniques. Good news preaching begins with the understanding that it is an absolute requirement for the sermon and that while scripture offers evidence of the revelation of God in human life, the source of the good news is God. A full description is provided in *Good News Preaching*[11]; however, the following is a summary of good news preaching:

- Is intentional about approaching and engaging the text with the expectation of finding good news.

- Brings to light the presence and grace of God visible in scripture in a way that connects with the context in which the sermon is preached.

- Offers the hearers a picture of divine grace that is actively transformative against the effects of human sin.

- Invites the hearers to receive and live into the active, transformative grace of God through a message that specifies the working of God's love in the hearts of all people that enables their discipleship in Christ.

Good news preaching interweaves the reality of human sin with the beneficence of God's free grace that is present and available for all people. The preacher interprets and interacts with the text in order to appropriate it for the context of the preached sermon, and regardless of the difficulty of a text, the offering of good news, however challenging for the preacher, must be identified, interpreted, and delivered in such a way that it will engage the hearts of the hearers and cause its application to effect transformation in the lives of the people.

Good news preaching does not require the sermon to be or to offer a sinecure for the troubles of life or of the world. What it does, or should do, is help the people of God to experience "the assurance of grace" that initiates or facilitates a change in the heart toward God, and supports one's discipleship in Christ.[12] It does not require a particular style of sermon or even of delivery. What it requires is a commitment on the part of the preacher to engage a homiletical process that reaches deeply beneath the layers of biblical text and congregational context to allow the light of divine grace to shine through the words of the sermon into the lives of the hearers. While each text may require its specific type of biblical interpretation and each context may make apparent different congregational issues, there is a simple methodology that may be followed in developing good news sermons from difficult texts.

THE METHODOLOGY

The methodological process for developing good news sermons from difficult texts contains four steps: analysis of the preaching context, interpretation of the biblical text, definition of the good news and the discipleship message, and creation of an expository sermon.[13]

Analysis of the Preaching Context

The preacher's first task is to analyze the context in which the sermon will be preached. In fact, more often than not, it is the preaching context that causes the difficulty in approaching the text for preaching. Assuredly there are certain biblical texts that simply by their contents are problematic for any context of preaching given our twenty-first-century, modern or postmodern, civilized Western culture. In such cases the historical analysis of the text must be given particular attention, but even then it does not override the analysis of the preaching context.

That the congregation has preconceived ideas about God and humanity is a foregone conclusion. And whether or not they have succumbed to the postmodern willingness to debunk the idea of the absolute truth of God or any aspect of humanity, they cannot but be impacted by society's fascination with the notion that all creation is theirs to revise, reshape, or reorder. How then does the text speak into that worldview? The approach to answering that essential homiletical question is to become as knowledgeable about the congregation as possible. Therefore analysis of the congregation is the essential first step in delivering good news from troublesome biblical texts.

Whether or not the preacher is also the pastor of the congregation, it is unlikely that the pastor/preacher has engaged in the type of congregational analysis described by Nancy T. Ammerman et al.[14] or Jackson W. Carroll and his group[15] in their work. In both cases their detailed study of congregations has delved into the systems and processes of congregations as they live out their identity as the beloved community. From a homiletical point of view, the analysis of the congregation centers more on their biblical, theological, and doctrinal beliefs and is the basis of the questions provided for the sermonic analysis. Appendix B provides a list of questions that may be used in the process of congregational analysis.

Interpretation of the Biblical Text

The second methodological step in the process of preaching good news from difficult texts is also one of contextual analysis. This analysis, however, is directed towards an exposition of the text. In the same way that the preacher engaged in a process of understanding the congregation, so also the preacher must understand the context of the scripture passage in order to appropriate its contents for preaching good news. Similar to the process outlined in *Good News Preaching*, the preacher does the work of interpreting the biblical text to understand the meaning of the text in its own context or contexts in order to particularize its relevance and applicability to the situation of preaching.

"Biblical exegesis is about offering a critical explanation of a biblical text. It requires that the reader delve deeply into the scripture passage to unearth its meaning."[16] Biblical exegesis or interpretation takes seriously and responds critically to the content of the biblical text so that the depth and the complexities of meaning and culture can be unearthed and applied in a way that brings to light the divine/human relationship that it represents. What the text meant and how it was received, understood, and used by the first hearers is as important as its meaning in the context in which it is located. Both levels of context and therefore of interpretation have relevance for the present reading and application.

This second step in the process is critical to good preaching, but even more so when the text is particularly challenging because it is so easy to misunderstand words when taken out of context. Whether they are used for good or ill, the words of scripture are more clearly of use and more valuable to the hearers when they accurately represent the meaning and use that they served in their original context. It is (hopefully) a safe assumption that a preacher who dares to select particularly difficult texts for preaching may be aware of the several interpretive tools that are available to engage the process of biblical interpretation. Whether or not the preacher has the training in ancient biblical languages, there are tools that are readily available to allow the preacher to reap the benefit of applying the embedded meaning to the present context. Appendix C provides a method for engaging simple biblical interpretation.

Definition of a Good News Statement and a Discipleship Message

The third step of the methodology brings us to the core of the endeavor. My thesis for preaching at all times is that it is the proclamation of the gospel. That gospel is the transformative good news of God's active engagement in human endeavors. As a Christian I know that Jesus Christ is the incarnation of God's unending love for humanity, yet preaching good news is not limited to offering them the person of Jesus Christ. As a trinitarian Christian, I hold that the offering of the gospel provides the opportunity to present the good news of God's love through the naming of God in all the persons of the Godhead and through the innumerable images that speak of the grace-full nature of God.

At this step the preacher identifies the good news, culled from the interpretation of the text that meets the needs of the waiting congregation. I hold fiercely and firmly to the belief that real good news is present, active, and transformative throughout scripture. And while it may be difficult to perceive in some texts, it is always present and available in the overarching story of God's covenantal love for humanity. Thus the preacher's responsibility is always to offer the good news of God's active presence in the midst of life's circumstances. Anything less is limited in its impact (if there is any impact at all) on the development of Christian discipleship in the hearts and lives of the hearers. Giving the congregation a definition of the nature of God, such as "God is love," or offering the promise of divine care in the future, such as "God will take care of you," is nearly always insufficient to meet the needs of the present. In most cases the hearers are seeking assurance of God's activity in the here and now, even as they hope for life in the future, as well as for their eternal life with Christ.

Real good news shows God actively present in the lives of the people. Previously I have directed preachers to begin the development of good news sermons by determining the good news of the text as the first step.[17] In the case of attempting to preach good news from difficult texts, determination of good news requires almost simultaneous consideration of context and text because of the critical nature of the interplay between the two. Consider the needs of the people as those needs connect with the contents or focus of the selected scripture passage. How and where do the two intersect? Assuming that the preacher has viable reasons for selecting the scripture passage (whether or not it is one of the lectionary texts) means that there was some reason or purpose for addressing the subject matter. That is the lead-in to the contents of the good news. Once the preacher has done the work of analyzing the context in detail, the requirements for the good news that should be gleaned from the contents of the biblical text engages the preacher's attention. Shaping the good news that speaks of God's transformative grace towards sinful humanity is this conjunction of the specific need of the context and the inherent response provided by the engagement of the text.

It is critical that the preacher resist the temptation to have the text say what seems to be required as evidence of the outpouring of God's grace. In order to be faithful to the text it will be necessary to include sufficient interpretive material so that the hearers can see the situation of the text more fully as they see God at work behind the scenes bringing about the work of restoration of humanity, which is the ultimate mission of the Divine. Faithfulness to the text in the identification of the good news is also critical because of the connection between the receipt of the good news and the work of discipleship. It is in the receipt of God's transformative action that the hearer is empowered to live the life and do the work of Christian discipleship. Thus in this third step, the preacher develops both a statement of good news and a discipleship message. The good news statement is a simple declarative statement with God as the subject, involved in the activity of transforming humanity, the receiver or beneficiary of God's action. An example of a good news statement may be: "God strengthens the weak." Although that statement is simple in structure, the preacher may yet struggle to discern the active work of God present and evidenced through the text. Following this good news, and given a situation where there is the issue of persons who have been led to engage in activities that are contrary to their Christian witness, the message of discipleship may be simply: "Go forward, trusting in God to sustain you."

Where the good news statement simply states God's actions in human lives, the message statement is directive and is intended to guide the hearers in Christian living. The message statement is always an imperative; however, the preacher must set aside all notions of coercing the hearers to act in specific ways considered to be for their good. The responsibility of the preacher is to proclaim good news and to help the congregation see how that good news can work in their lives for their living as Christians. Thus, although the message statement is offered as a command, it should be considered more in the nature as an imperative that may encourage the hearers to live out their Christian commitment and not an order from the preacher to take specific action or perform specific acts as a recompense for God's action in their lives. Appendix D provides guidelines for creating the good news and message statements.

Creation of the Sermon

The fourth and final step in the process is the framing of the sermon. In order to preach good news from any text, one must engage the text. The sermon may be expository, focusing almost myopically on the specific text, or topical, serving as foundational scripture for the particular focus of a sermon. Because of the troublesome nature of some texts, using them for a topical sermon may shift the focus from the topic to the text as the preacher is forced to give those texts special attention and emphasis so that they can speak appropriately to the context of the sermon. Thus it is more appropriate, and possibly easier, to use difficult Bible passages in an expository sermon.

Scripture is the foundation for all sermons, whether expository or topical. There is redundancy inherent in the term "biblical sermon" that compounds the misunderstanding that sermons are anything but biblical. When preachers decide to engage a particular topic for preaching, one aspect of that task is to select passages of scripture that provide appropriate biblical support for whatever aspect of the topic they seek to engage. As stated earlier, wisdom directs the preacher to avoid recognizably difficult texts in support of a chosen topic. To do otherwise may require giving so much attention to the difficult text that the focus of the sermon is moved from the selected topic to the specific text. Expository preaching allows the preacher to focus on a chosen text. The style of the sermon may be one of many appropriate sermonic structures,[18] but all are intended to give light to the meaning of the text in the life of the hearers and particularly to bring to life the divine action of transformative grace for the good of individuals and the community.

An important caveat about this methodology is that it does not prevent the mishandling of difficult biblical texts. From the beginning of the Christian era there has been misreading of biblical stories, such that many passages of scripture have been used to justify oppression and injustice of all kinds. In too many cases the good news of the gospel has been offered to some at the expense of others. Countless preachers have, in their sermons, withheld the free grace of God from those they have considered unworthy. And even in this postmodern era of the twenty-first century, the church has been engaged in "othering" selected groups of persons and has used scripture to support its stance and actions. Preaching good news from difficult texts appropriately is not the function of this methodology, no matter how precisely it is followed. It is, rather, the responsibility of the preacher, who must take seriously the reality of the grace-full word of God that is embedded in scripture, and who diligently engages the process that unearths that divine word and then offers it with care to the waiting congregation.

NAMING THE TROUBLE IN THE TEXT

As stated earlier, there are many biblical stories and situations that are difficult for preachers. Following are brief descriptions of the four genres of trouble that are addressed in this work, in the sequence that they appear in chapters 2 to 5, as named:

1. A Troublesome God—Some texts reveal a characteristic of the nature of God that is fickle, unjust, punitive, prejudiced, and perhaps even racist. These qualities are contrary to what one expects of the loving God most Christians have been taught to worship, and these texts are thus problematic to preach.

2. In the Family of God—Here the focus is family systems represented in the biblical narrative, either through those who are recognized as the chosen people of God or through familial situations presented in biblical stories told by Jesus. At times family dynamics result in pain and violence, and biblical models that are representative of divine approbation make it difficult for preachers to use such texts in some congregational settings.

3. For the Sake of the Community—The church as the beloved community is the hope of every church pastor. It is the model of corporate Christian witness and the location of social holiness that is the hoped for goal when the people of God gather. When dysfunction occurs in communities, both clergy and lay people may look to the Bible for direction. Texts that seem to support, model, or encourage such dysfunction present a serious challenge for preachers.

4. Living a Holy Life—Preaching holiness as a standard for Christians offers a challenge for preachers, given the prevailing world culture. Living a life that personifies the righteousness of

God, in a world that decries many Christian values as foolish, makes preaching such texts difficult for the preacher and also difficult for the congregation to hear and accept.

The trouble named may originate from the contents of the text or the context of the congregation, but whatever the difficulty, the preacher's responsibility—to seek the divine grace that surrounds the troublesome Bible story—is to offer good news on every occasion of preaching. Reaching into and beyond the difficulties necessitates interpretive action, belief in the divine covenant, and prayerful imagination that engages the heart and mind of both preacher and people.

· 2 ·

A TROUBLESOME GOD

FEARFUL OR FEARED?

*The Lord came down to see the city and the tower, which mortals
had built. And the Lord said, "Look, they are one people, and they
have all one language; and this is only the beginning of what they
will do; nothing that they propose to do will now be impossible
for them. Come, let us go down, and confuse their language there,
so that they will not understand one another's speech." So the Lord
scattered them abroad from there over the face of all the earth, and
they left off building the city. (Gen. 11:5–8)*

As one views the current condition of the world and the distance created between people who do not have a common language, it seems
appropriate to interrogate this text as to the divine motivation for
God's action, but in my estimation a greater question is located in
the area of theodicy. What in the nature of God is so fragile that God
cannot allow the people that God created to unite in building a tower
and sharing a common language, which would also be a uniting force?

Questions such as these are common ones that bedevil preachers who have approached this text and others like it, questions that seem to present a troublesome picture of God. In the midst of a world culture of excess, where building bigger and better breadboxes is desired and lauded by much of humanity, the idea that God would object to such industriousness on the part of human beings is a difficult concept that would be received negatively by most, if not all, congregations in the United States. Industry is a motif of modern living, fueled by the belief that "bigger is better" and the so-called Protestant work ethic. The propensity for segregating ourselves along divisions of race, clan, and language is a prevalent theme in modern and postmodern society. Particularly because of this, a surface reading of this text does not immediately provide good news for preaching.

The situation of the text seems to present a picture of unity, the like of which the world with all its divisions and the hierarchies supported by said divisions could use to its great benefit. Moreover, the words of the text seem to suggest that God is the victim of fear, and, worse yet, the reason for that fear is human power. The question of theodicy has engaged theologians for centuries since the term was first coined by philosopher Gottfried Leibniz[1] in 1710 and requires much more scrutiny than that afforded to a preacher who has the responsibility of preaching a text each week in the midst of the day-to-day administration and the pastoral care of a waiting congregation. But the preacher is nevertheless left with a text for preaching that presents, to the congregation if not to the preacher, a picture of a God who is afraid or challenged by the power of the very ones God created. Or the text may leave both preacher and congregation with the unsettling feeling that God, like an unruly child, is not only prone to tantrums that are potentially destructive to the created order but, worse yet, is also given to finding devious ways to undermine the industriousness and creativity of humanity.

Consider the magnitude of the challenge in the face of a tsunami and subsequent radiation meltdown that impacted the people of Japan in 2011, or the devastating earthquake in Haiti in 2010, or Hurricane Katrina and its aftermath of broken levees, or the 2009 tsunami in Indonesia that took more than 200,000 lives. The preacher is confronted by the realities of life in the present, the over-whelming need of the people to experience a living reality of divine grace, and a text that seems to offer anything but grace or even a pic-ture of the divine/human relationship that is representative of a loving God. This text is at best a homiletical challenge, and the search for good news must be undertaken with intensity and great depth.

The secret of God's nature evident in this text is embedded in the context of the whole story of creation. God is concerned about human development and the building of the Tower of Babel speaks more about human arrogance and the need for power than it does of indus-try. God had commanded human beings—offered a divine invitation for humanity to partner with God in creation—to be fruitful and fill the earth. Human desire has taken a different trajectory and is aimed at consolidating humans' power in one place. By stopping their early efforts, God advances the created order according to God's plan. The preacher must carefully construct the message so that the congrega-tion can see the guiding hand of God at work both to prevent human beings from straying further from the path of life in community and to lead them in the way that is meant to bring fullness of life.

While that may be the summative conclusion of the story, how can the people hear it, given the context of their lives? But there are more elements to the difficulty than the text alone. The context of their lives has conditioned most congregations to believe in the effi-cacy of industriousness as the key to happiness. An analysis of the congregational culture in the midst of a capitalist society can reveal the people's expectations of reward for any effort expended. It is part and parcel of who they are and, despite any touting of the transfor-mation of Christians by Christ and their disinclination to conform to world's standards, the reality is that even in the church one expects to be commended for work done to advance society as one conceives it. The preacher, who is also a member of the society, is faced with difficulty in both text and context. And given that it is unlikely that said preacher can change society with a single sermon, the preacher's focus centers on the text.

In order to see fully into the text and discern the grace it offers, the preacher approaches the text with expectation of seeing God's grace revealed in action with human beings. Despite the difficulty the text may present, the preacher is charged with offering good news and embodying that good news as present reality. Appropriate exegetical steps must be taken to overcome the difficulty without dismissing the details presented or ignoring the ramifications of the challenge or whitewashing the real meaning and the theological implications inherent in both text and context. Understanding that the good news for the present moment of preaching is not limited to the specific divine/human interaction revealed by a single text. It offers an opportunity to go behind, beneath, or beyond the selected passage to unearth the specifics of divine action for the present.

Another reality that the text reveals and delivers in the midst of the context is human diversity. At a time in history where people of different languages in society are seen and treated as other, the idea that God intended the world to be a place of differences among people—of multiple languages, cultures, and colors—is one that deserves attention as it speaks of God's grace freely offered to all. Many churches still struggle with the issue of new neighbors in established churches and communities. Some balk, while others hope for the construct of their community to depict a multicultural motif. Still others pray for continued homogeneity as they hold on to a past long gone. The Tower of Babel story may offer a path to addressing the contextual problem of opening hearts and doors to the divine vision of many races, many languages, and many peoples. It is difficult, but it is good news for preaching, as it depicts an image of the realm of God where God reigns as sovereign over all the peoples of the earth.

WORSHIP OR SACRIFICE?

Understanding that the good news of the biblical text, anchored in past events and descriptive of a reality that is far removed from the present, is witness to the timelessness of God's grace enables the preacher to move the action of God forward and allow it to be substantive in the present. The familiar story of Abraham and Isaac and God's call for the sacrifice of Isaac presents a troubling picture of God as desirous of murderous sacrifice.

After these things God tested Abraham. He said to him, "Abra-
ham!" And he said, "Here I am." He said, "Take your son, your
only son Isaac, whom you love, and go to the land of Moriah, and
offer him there as a burnt offering on one of the mountains that I
shall show you." (Gen. 22:1–2)

To most parents, it is an unfathomable request. The text describes it
as a test, but why is this type of horrific test necessary? The idea of
human sacrifice is abhorrent to our twenty-first-century Western
minds, but not so in Abraham's time. Yet what seems truly unfathomable is that God would require the sacrifice of the same son
through whom the promise of posterity has been promised to Abraham and Sarah. What is it in the nature of God that would require
such absolute worship to the point of sacrifice? That seems to be the
most troubling question in this text.

Scripture facilitates the revelation of God's eternal covenantal
love for humanity, and because of its familiarity and the fact that we
are inheritors of the Abrahamic covenant, the intensity of the event
narrated in the text has lost some of its sting. That too often causes
preachers to rush to the ending where Isaac is saved and a ram is sacrificed in its stead without lingering in the details and allowing the
complete news of divine love to surface and have its full impact on
the hearers. Regardless of the specific context of the congregation, it
is doubtful that the idea of sacrificing one's child will be given serious
consideration by congregants. But, depending on the congregation,
the preacher may be faced with the difficult task of revealing the
many instances of children being "sacrificed" by parents so that they
can pursue the upward mobility of societal success. In such cases there
is no available "ram" to take the place of the relationship that is forever lost in the search for more of what life seems to be offering. It
is a difficult message for most preachers, and may require their own
type of sacrifice.

Unfortunately, that leads to the story being preached simply as
evidence that God always provides (a ram in the thicket). There is
also difficulty in preaching about the sacrifices that we are called to
make in order to live fully Christian lives. For many, the idea of giving

totally of one's substance or even offering one's best to God calls for a depth of faith that they do not have or cannot reach. Given the state of many churches, it does not require proven statistics (although they exist) to show that giving one's all or even one's best to God is not practiced by a majority of people. And yet, despite this, God continues to provide for the needs of the people. The difficulty in the text is no greater than the difficulty in the context where sacrificial faith is in short supply and where the expectation of God's provision is considered an intrinsic right of human life.

The overarching message of scripture, contained in both the Old and the New Testaments, is the constancy of God's covenantal love for humanity. With this foundational belief as the backdrop, this text takes on a new and different meaning. The preacher who approaches this story of human sacrifice with that basic understanding cannot help but begin with the recognition of good news that is more than the saving of the life of one child. It is the saving of the covenantal relationship between God and the people of God that is thus allowed to take its rightful place in center stage. It is the reality of divine love that enlivens, awakens, and energizes preacher and people for joyful, sacrificial living even in a troubled world.

God's call for sacrifice is not an aberration in the nature of God but an invitation to faithfulness beyond the limits that we place on our lives. The preacher is not simply called to retrieve the good news, in this case by rushing to find the ram in the bushes, but must struggle to decipher it in the midst of unfathomable and sometimes incomprehensible biblical language and challenging or even overwhelming life situations. Often the task is time-consuming and frustrating; but consider the reward of seeing the joy that lights up the face and ultimately the life of even one person who, confronted by his or her own challenges of sacrifice, experiences redemption, relief, and new life by being connected to the source of good news through the sermon.

The source of the good news is always God, and the preacher's task and responsibility is to point the people to God through the sermon. The moral dilemma in the text is one that is faced by Christians, clergy and lay people alike, even though the particularities of each situation may be different. Theodore Hiebert in an excursus on this text offers two common responses: "According to one, God is above all human moral codes and is free to act in divine wisdom: God's ways are not human ways. According to the other, the vast difference between ancient and modern cultural norms (and their accompanying theologies) must be emphasized and incorporated into any contemporary response."[2] While both responses are appropriate in some sense, neither offers the preacher substantive good news to be shared with the community and in fact point to other types of difficulty for the preacher.

The parent whose child has been stricken with a mortal illness, or who has lost a family member, especially a young person, through tragic circumstances or in the armed services, is not helped by the seemingly facile response to their situation as they see it revealed in the text. Their child was not saved by divine intervention and in fact to their minds God was both uncaring and absent from their particular situation. Why was their experience one of sacrificial giving? Why was God absent from their situation? Why was there no redemption for their child? What then is the good news that this troublesome picture of God requires or permits?

The challenge of homiletical exegesis required for such texts is intensified by a level of biblical interpretation that is often more suited to biblical scholars than to ordinary preachers. In addition to detailed, in-depth work, the preacher must prayerfully seek divine guidance, since God is the ultimate source of the good news.

> It is God working through the text to untangle the good news from the often convoluted streams of text and historical contexts; God working through the preacher to disengage beliefs and biases and to destroy filters that misappropriate or misinterpret the words of scripture; and God working through the people in the present and active contexts of their individual and corporate lives to bring to their attention the revelation and assurance of divine grace.[3]

Through the analysis of the congregation, the preacher, aware of the special needs of congregants, may choose to focus more on the continued presence of God with Abraham at that most difficult moment. On another occasion the message of Abraham's faithfulness to God (hopefully preached through a different text, such as Hebrews 11) may be of more value to the congregation in support of their own faith. But where there is still the pain of loss present with the people, the good news of God's enduring presence would be more appropriate than either the issue of divine right or human faithfulness. At all times the good news must be viable in order for it to be a source of transformation in the lives of the people.

Elizabeth Achtemeier reminds us that God's testing of Abraham is a major theme of this text and that "[W]e must not water down that assertion. God's promise of blessing for the world rides on the faith and obedience of Abraham, who has been chosen to be the medium of blessing."[4] Her point is important in the face of the need to offer good news to the people. To reiterate a key point of *Good News Preaching*, finding and offering authentic good news requires that the preacher engage the exegetical process with integrity. Just as each sermon is preached in a particular context, so also each scripture text is representative of a particular biblical context. Given that the creation of the biblical record was not done in real time, the scripture passage is connected to multiple historical contexts, all of which may have significance in deciphering its meaning and claiming its good news for the present. Achtemeier's warning with respect to the motif of trust that is a recognizable theme in this text reminds us of the need for proper interpretation. "We must not think, however, that God's test of our trust in him is behind every single affliction that we suffer. In the Scriptures, God tests his servants when his purposes are at stake."[5] Her analysis rests on the Judeo-Christian belief that Abraham is the channel of blessing for the nations of the world, and given the context in which this text was developed, it was important or even a necessity for the people to whom it was written to receive the witness of God's promise through them, the descendents of Abraham.[6] The difficulty of preaching this difficult Bible passage is thus mitigated by the reality of God's presence in the context of both the text and the present.

DIVINE SELECTION OR FAVORITISM?

The issue of trust in God is one that is present in much of scripture even as it is representative of the covenantal relationship between God and the people of God in scripture and in the world. The journey of the Hebrew people to become the people of Israel took them through more than flooded seas and parched deserts in their effort to reach the promised land. It was essentially a journey of faith that called for belief in a God that they did not know fully and who seemed to require more of them than they could give. The God of the journey seemed to demand a level of faith and obedience that if disobeyed resulted in the wrath of God being brought upon the people. It is an aspect of the nature of God that has been exploited by some preachers whose theology rests on the notion of God as punishing sovereign.

> *The people spoke against God and against Moses, "Why have you brought us up out of Egypt to die in the wilderness? For there is no food and no water, and we detest this miserable food." Then the Lord sent poisonous serpents among the people and they bit the people, so that many Israelites died. (Num. 21:5–6)*

"Why is God making us suffer like this?" It is the cry of many who find themselves in death-dealing situations. The economic crises in the United States that came to full bloom in 2009 and 2010 caused many people to cry out to and against God. Some were Christians, and others who had not previously given open allegiance to any specific deity suddenly found themselves reaching out to or challenging the higher power that they believed had control of their lives.

The cover of Mario Puzo's book *The Godfather* shows the picture of a hand in control of several figures that hang from a frame. It portrays the Godfather as a puppet master with the people under his control operating like puppets at his behest. In many ways God is considered by many people, even Christians, to be a divine puppet master who controls people at God's whim. As a result when bad things happen it is easy, and in their minds appropriate, to blame God for what has occurred. In those moments it is God who did, who sent, who withheld, or who denied. In the moment of their tragedy God is seen as whimsical, fickle, or even evil and the goodness of God is dismissed or considered unfathomable. In such instances no responsibility is attributed to human decisions or actions. God is given the blame for all that has gone wrong.

In the report of Israel's situation, being overrun by poisonous snakes, the writer or writers of the book of Numbers put the responsibility for the calamity solidly on God. God has sent the snakes as punishment to the people because they have complained against God and against Moses, the man chosen by God to lead the people. What does this text say to us about the nature of God, and how does it translate into good news for the people of God today? The text almost invites abuse (and has been used in such a way) by those who would take an autocratic stance in their leadership role. Interpreted in the context of dictatorial leadership, it can be used as a whip or an instrument of fear to repress followers. In the full story of the encounter, there is the requisite good news. The people confess their sinfulness and appeal to Moses to speak to God on their behalf; Moses prays to God; God hears and provides a cure for those who have been bitten but have not yet succumbed to the poison in their system. This good news does little, however, to redeem the erroneous interpretation named previously. So how does this story translate for today's church? Can it be preached as a good news sermon?

The premise that every sermon must offer the good news of God's transformative love active in human lives, a tenet of my homiletical/liturgical theology, speaks to an important aspect of the essential nature of the word being proclaimed in worship and not the word as worship. The worship of the people of God is a doxological response to God's ongoing and unending grace. When the object of worship deviates from God to the words of scripture, such that the words themselves are considered the Word of God, problems of understanding and focus arise that may circumvent the true worship of God. Such a situation has been true for this text, and it has led some Christians, even in this twenty-first century, to preach that natural disasters or events that are not directly or specifically of human creation, and that result in pain, suffering, or death, are the direct punishment of God for sins that have been committed. In some cases where even babies or young children are concerned, the belief is that such hardship originates from God and fits with the punitive nature of God.

Preachers who offer such reasoning, who, as a whole genre of preaching is wont to do, represent God as the arbiter of pain and damnation, misrepresent the true nature of God. It is not only a misreading of scripture, but also of God. It is the same misreading that leads some Christian preachers to preach fire and destruction on those who do not follow their narrow reading of scripture. The nature of God as not only omnipotent and omniscient but as involved in and directing all of life may in part be responsible for this misrepresentation of God. This misinterpretation has been and continues to be prevalent in Christianity and makes a difficult text even more so as the preacher considers how best to apply the story to the people's lives. If the culture of the community is such that every event, whether good or ill, is attributed to God's direct action, that complicates the task of preaching this story in a way that reveals the true picture of divine grace. The preacher cannot selectively choose which action of God is correctly attributable to God and which is not. The text states that it is God who sends the serpents and there is no avoiding that issue. It should not be used, however, as the definitive model of God's interaction with human beings and particularly human sinfulness. Juxtaposing human sin and divine grace in a credible way is essential to revealing the true nature of God as the source of good news.

Generally this text from Numbers is presented alongside the New Testament text that compares the lifting of the bronze snake that Moses is commanded to make and use as a curative for the snakebitten Israelites with Jesus lifted on the cross. The preacher can thus bypass the difficulty of dealing with the problem of God who punishes. On the other hand, scholars have sought to resolve the challenge of this particular text by stressing the twofold nature of the serpents or seraphim—punishment and healing. Because the text does not allow ambivalence in identifying God as the source of Israel's punishment, the preacher must also admit to the nature of suffering by those who voluntarily walk away from God. The good news of the sermon occurs always at the juxtaposition of sin and grace, where God's grace mitigates human sin. Human sin may have caused pain and death, but God's redeeming love has offered restoration of life. The sermon and its good news thus takes its rightful place in the worship experience as it engages the people in recognizing and celebrating God's restorative and transforming presence in the midst of trouble. The scriptures offer many examples, as can be found in this text, of God's presence and power operating in the lives of people to bring about restoration from trouble.

TRIAL OR TRUST?

One example of such trouble and restoration is found in the story of Job. In Sunday school I learned the phrase "patient like Job," but closer reading and study revealed a man, Job, who turned out to be not as patient as he was touted to be. The mystery of Job's situation is also the mystery of a gambler God who wreaks havoc or allows Satan to wreak havoc on Job's life. When Job's wife advises him to "curse God and die" (Job 2:9b) she does so out of a sense of compassion for his suffering. That he does not take his wife's advice speaks strongly for Job's faith in God and his understanding and commitment to his relationship with God. Even when he challenges God, it demonstrates his continued relationship with God. The issue for many who suffer, however, is not whether like Job they can hold fast to their faith. It is why they should be required to suffer in the first place. It is little wonder that Job's story is not a favorite for preachers (at least not for the preachers I know) because it is difficult to find divine love in an account that begins with God allowing tragedy of immense proportions to overtake the life of one of God's faithful servants merely on a whim.

The book has earned scholarly approbation as one of the finest if not the "finest wisdom text of the Jewish and Christian canons."[7] The preacher's first challenge is perhaps explaining the difference between Satan, the devil, and Ha-Satan, one of God's messengers who initiates the bet with God that puts Job at the center of a whirlwind of destruction in his life. Expositors and commentators focus on the text as concerned with the issue of divine justice, but the reading of these texts in the congregation places it at the heart of many people's questions about the nature of God. And the conclusion, based on God's actions, is troublesome.

> *One day the heavenly beings came to present themselves before the Lord, and Satan also came among them to present himself before the Lord. The Lord said to Satan, "Where have you come from?" Satan answered the Lord, "From going to and fro on the earth and from walking up and down on it." The Lord said to Satan, "Have you considered my servant Job? There is no one like him on the earth, a blameless and upright man who fears God and turns away from evil. He still persists in his integrity, although you incited me against him, to destroy him for no reason." Then Satan answered the Lord, "Skin for skin! All that people have they will give to save their lives. But stretch out your hand now and touch his bone and his flesh, and he will curse you to your face." The Lord said to Satan, "Very well, he is in your power, only spare his life." (Job 2:1–6)*

What does one do with a God who brings havoc to the life of God's faithful? In my time as a pastor, I have been asked more than once, Why did God let all this happen to Job? For the ordinary person in the pew the question "Why do bad things happen to good people?" is not the one that is on their lips. That, for many, is an academic debate that does not speak to the emotional and spiritual agony of losing trust in God and becoming blind to the goodness of God. Carol A. Newsom suggests:

> To the reader who is willing to forgo simplistic answers, however, the book offers a challenging exploration of religious issues of fundamental importance: the motivation for piety, the meaning of suffering, the nature of God, the place of justice in the world, and the relationship of order and chaos in God's design of creation.[8]

But the man and woman in the pew caught in a vicious cycle of unrelieved suffering are not prone to such a "challenging exploration" of the text. Their concern and their cry, much like Job's eventually, is to God. Why? Why, God? In other words: Who are you and where are you, God? Not only is God responsible for the tragedy, but to them God is absent in the midst of the greatest tragedy of their lives.

The situation of this context seems to cry out for an assurance of God's loving care. But in the book of Job, the trouble originates from God. Unlike Abraham, Job is not in the essential covenantal line, so why the test? To my mind, there is no easy answer for any congregation. It does not help that the story belongs to the genre of myth. To adapt a phrase from the vernacular of the African American church: "That does not preach." When people consider the vagaries of society where some have great success and others have greater troubles or disappointments, reverting the scholarly interpretive devices or conclusions is not the appropriate way to deal with the difficulty of this text. The preacher is well advised to admit to the incomprehensibility of the text and bring alive the interaction between God and Job in the midst of Job's trouble. Yet even there, the good news seems sparse. God responds to Job with a divine challenge, so that despite the relationship between the two protagonists, God's sovereignty over Job is clearly articulated. And although Job experiences restoration, it seems insufficient to overcome the sense of betrayal that is felt at God's action towards Job. It is difficult to celebrate good news on the basis of this text alone.

How does doxological worship come forth in such a calamitous situation? What does the preacher say in the midst of abject suffering? More importantly for this homiletical engagement, what's the good news from this text? Students who have been confronted with preaching texts from this book have come into my office bewildered by my insistence that they find transformative good news for preaching. Even untutored as many of the beginning preachers are, they understand that racing to the end of the story where all is restored is not the answer. In real life, the dead are still gone from the midst. The grief of loss is still a present reality despite the signs of restoration. And the difficulty of the situation compounds the difficulty of preaching good news from this text.

Recently I saw a story in which a couple's three children were killed in an accident. In the face of such devastating loss, they decided to reverse the process they had taken to prevent pregnancy once they had considered their family complete after the birth of their third child. Miraculously, not only did the procedure work, but the result was triplets, two girls and a boy, as they had previously. The couple was clear that while they rejoiced in the new children, in no way were they restoration of the first three. They were additions, because the first three still lived in their hearts. So the preacher that offers the hearers the panacea of divine restoration of what they had before their tragedy misses the real good news of God's presence in the midst of the tragedy.

Our relationship with God is an act of grace that sustains us through our times of trouble. It is divine grace alone, operating in the heart and the words of the preacher, that will bring to light for the hearers the grace of God that places assurance in the faith of his servant Job as he continues to hold fast to his belief in God. The preacher may also offer as divine grace the reality of God's personal knowledge of Job. Beginning with the original dialogue with Satan, God knew Job. And God knew how Job had responded to Satan's first dastardly acts. Even when Job's friends try to convince him that his sinfulness has caused his troubles; even when Job rails against God because of his inability to comprehend his situation; even when God snaps back at Job—an abiding truth is that God knows Job personally. The evidence of God's personal knowledge of human beings may be appropriate good news depending on the context, particularly as it relates to God's action of support for our lives.

The mystery of God's original action towards Job remains just that, and the preacher should resist trying to be the one who alone knows the mind of God and be authentic, even to the unwelcome task of admitting lack of knowledge of either the text or the purposes of God. The troublesome nature of God, who seems to act on a whim, opening one of God's faithful servants to Satan's manipulative actions, is as hard to explain as God's call for the sacrifice of Isaac. But, as in that story, the reality of God's active, redemptive, restorative presence is the sermonic good news that must be preached in a way that can not only touch, but permeate, the hurting places of one's inner being. The challenge of Job, who sits literally in a place of trouble, on a dung heap, and the preacher's response of God's ongoing relationship and presence with Job as divine grace enables the preacher to assume a rightful place in the gathering of those who dare to speak for God.

THE VOICE OF GOD OR THE PROPHET'S DILEMMA?

The preacher, at his or her authentic best, speaks for God and in so doing takes on the role of prophet. Every preacher is called to be prophetic. Prophetic preaching as a homiletical genre is much touted and attributed at times to an elite minority whose voices have resounded in tall-steeple churches or other places of ecclesial might and power. It is my contention that every event of authentic preaching is prophetic. The prophet is one who speaks for God, and every person who claims the title of preacher can do so authentically and with integrity only if that person does so in the name of God and by the power of the Holy Spirit. The words of the preacher become the Word of God only through the presence and empowering grace of the Holy Spirit. Thus everyone who speaks the Word of God—who in effect speaks for God, who becomes God's mouthpiece—speaks prophetically and is thus engaged in prophetic preaching.

More than any other person in biblical history, the prophet speaks in the midst of the gathered community. Likewise the preacher proclaims the Word of God to the people gathered in the name of Jesus Christ. The people gather for worship and praise to God, and preaching is thus a liturgical act that achieves authenticity when performed in the midst of the people. The prophets of biblical antiquity were recognized as speaking for God and to that end they offered a picture of God that was not always comforting. When the prophet delivered a message from God, the people responded, or not, with the understanding that the recipient of their response was God. The postexilic writings that represent the biblical heritage of the Christian faith reveal a picture of a God who had a punitive side that encouraged war and retributive justice. It is a picture of God that various groups throughout Christendom have used to mete out punishment and what might be called punitive justice in the name of God.

But it is not only the people on whom God's judgment falls. Prophets are subject to punishment for subverting the Word of God. Here also is a troublesome picture of God.

> *When this people, or a prophet, or a priest asks you, "What is the burden of the Lord?" you shall say to them, "You are the burden, and I will cast you off, says the Lord." And as for the prophet, priest, or the people who say, "The burden of the Lord," I will punish them and their households. (Jer. 23:33–34)*

This is not a particularly familiar text, and perhaps that is because it would be difficult for most preachers to preach. This text reminds us that it is not only the people on whom God's punitive judgment falls. Preachers are subject to punishment for subverting the Word of God. The preacher of this text is confronted not only with the possibility of an indictment against her or his own preaching, since it is condemning of false prophets, or perhaps more appropriately for the present context, preachers who claim to preach in the name of God and offer nothing of substance. But even if the preacher feels justified and considers the indictment to be against other preachers, because it is God who metes out the punishment, and because the New Testament directive of Christ speaks against judging others, the preacher is caught between a rock and a hard place in the effort to avoid divine punishment.

So is there good news for prophet-preachers in this text? Since theirs is the task and responsibility of offering the transformative grace of God for the life of the people, there would be justifiable expectation that the prophets would adhere to God's directives for their own life and work. So why does there need to be such harsh punishment? What is the nature of God that necessitates that? The culture in which we live makes those questions somewhat normative. Persons who do their job according to its requirements want to be rewarded and those who do not generally do not consider the breaking of the implied or even explicit covenant cause for much concern and certainly not for punishment. And yet there is the warning that this text brings, and perhaps that is the good news for preachers. God lays out the requirements and provides specifics on the punishment that attends nonadherence. That is realistic good news; there can be no unexpected results. God guides our future by providing the guidelines by which we are to live and do the work of God. It is clear evidence of the foundational good news of God's empowering grace in the continuing covenantal relationship with humanity. It is proof of the assurance of God's continued favor. The challenge for preachers is to apply those guidelines to themselves, rather than claiming the right to judge others by their interpretation and thus subverting the inherent good news.

THE REVELATION OF GRACE

For Christians, the redemptive act of Jesus Christ recorded in scripture is the epitome of good news. Jesus in his time on earth was the tangible revelation of God's love, and thus representative of God's grace for all time and all people. And yet here also we find what seems like a human flaw in divine form.

> *Now the woman was a Gentile, of Syrophoenician origin. She begged him to cast out the demon out of her daughter. He said to her, "Let the children be fed first, for it is not fair to take the children's food and throw it to the dogs." (Mark 7:26–27)*

So God is racist? That's a big problem! And the good news of the text is that the woman persists and Jesus gives in? What's so good about that? Who needs a God that marginalizes the marginalized? The scholarship that surrounds the meaning of this text is complicated and difficult to preach. There are many suggestions about the connection of the interaction between Jesus and the Gentile woman and its analogous relationship to the mission to the Gentiles. There is also a somewhat convoluted explanation offered about product grown by Jewish peasant farmers and sent to the cities, leaving the farmers in want. But neither of these preaches well in the face of what has become common knowledge, namely that the term "dogs" used as it was represented a racial slur.

The society of the United States and certainly its Christian churches are still clearly divided along racial lines. A president who is African American has brought to light the inherent racism of society as many in power have focused and pooled their efforts to bring him down even at the expense of their careers or of the people that they have sworn to represent. New immigration laws have been put in place that are clearly along racial lines as some have determined to keep their society "pure." In the recent past, public commentators have run afoul of their employers, although only for limited periods and at little cost in most cases, for using racial slurs in public forums. And there is Jesus, the incarnate God, caught putting down one of the very ones he has come to save, and doing so by using racialized language. Where's the transformative grace of God in such action?

An analysis of the particular context of preaching may not immediately reveal the reality of the racism that is still an unfinished agenda for the church even as it is in the world. Even where the congregation boasts of a multicultural makeup, the pastor is well served by looking closely at the seating pattern of members in worship. The preacher is also advised to look deeply and honestly into her or his own heart to unearth the hidden prejudices that rise unbidden in unexpected situations and events. The challenges inherent in the wider community of society and the world also creep into the interactions between persons in the beloved community at every level of engagement. Admitting the underlying presence of issues such as race, gender, sexual orientation, class, and all disabilities that name persons in our sphere as "other" is a necessary beginning point for offering good news from this text or any other biblical text. It claims the reality of life that is challenging in expected and unexpected ways.

Perhaps seeing the exchange between Jesus and the Syrophoenician woman in a different light might enable the preacher to offer distinctive good news in which God in Christ is still the subject. What occurs in this text is Jesus' challenge to the woman. Her retort and the subsequent engagement between the two strengthen the woman to hold fast to the personhood that proclaims her humanity and her identity as a child of God. As redeemed children of God we face challenges that would demean or even deny our full identity in Christ. If Christ himself is willing to allow the woman to challenge him, we are also strengthened to challenge all the forces that come against us and that would deny us the rights we have as children of God.

Challenges similar to this biblical woman's are part of my story as a black woman of some middle years. The knowledge of Christ's redemptive, empowering grace is often the source of the strength that enables me to stand firm against the people, systems, and forces that would demean or seek to destroy the inner core of my being. And my story is not unique. The Syrophoenician woman's story is the story of women and minority race persons within and outside the church. It is the story of any person who would be named "other" and therefore considered less by some dominant group. Preaching good news from this text calls for encouraging strength through Christ that enables all people to face down the prejudices of their situation whenever and however they are challenged.

Given the context of the story, it is feasible to accept that Jesus was not only challenging the woman to claim her rights but also challenging the minds of the disciples who would have disdained to have the woman in their presence. Does that mean that we are permitted to allow others to be demeaned in order to teach them Christ's lesson of acceptance? I think not. Instead, we are called to recognize and denounce any action that would make others less than we are and stand up for the rights of others to live as God intended, as the persons of full worth that they are.

Certainly, Jesus went to great pains to reach out to many in society who were considered other. Among his disciples he numbered a tax collector, among his friends he counted lepers, and within his company he included many women. The temple leaders did not understand him and even his disciples missed the point as they questioned his association with persons that their society considered outcast. And yet there were moments when his response to the very ones he later accepted seems questionable.

Jesus said to her, "Go call your husband, and come back." The woman answered him, "I have no husband." ... Jesus said to her, "You are right in saying 'I have no husband'; for you have had five husbands and the one you have now is not your husband. What you have said is true!" The woman said to him, "Sir, I see that you are a prophet." (John 4:16–19)

This short piece of the dialog between the Samaritan woman at the well and Jesus has been the cause of many misogynistic sermons, and some of those from women preachers. It is always surprising to me when women preachers follow their male colleagues in condemning the woman for her many husbands and her common-law husband (to use a term of my birth culture). What is worse for me is that my years of teaching have revealed that 99 percent of the time African American preachers in my classes are the ones who immediately attack the character of the woman. Given the context of their history in the United States of America, one would assume (I certainly did) that they would understand the fragility of life for one who was cast off and see in her situation the same situation that confronts many single women in their culture. But here also they are affected by the hegemonic influences of the culture of society in the United States, which plays a part in directing the appropriation of this text for preaching and helps to detract from its offering of good news.

In the midst of guiding the students to exegete the historical context more accurately, I am often left wondering why it was even necessary for this piece of conversation to be engaged by Jesus, since it has done so much harm to the woman's reputation over time. New Testament scholars consider it simply a sign of Jesus' prophetic identity. There is no evidence that Jesus' response was in any way condemnatory, but the misrepresentation of this text by preachers may raise the question of its necessity in light of the harm that it has engendered over the centuries of the church. And although this small piece of the text is not normally segregated for reading in the congregation, too often it is the only part of the story emphasized, and it is preached as anything but good news for women.

Although most women in today's society in the United States are generally not subject to the vagaries of marital support nor are they subject to the Levirate laws that some New Testament scholars consider might have been one reason for the many marriages, the erroneous conclusion of moral laxity on the part of the woman often clouds the good news of this text. When it is read that Jesus saved her from a life of sexual immorality, it can sound a condemnatory or dismissive note in the ears of women who have been married more than once, or who may be in a partnership relationship outside of marriage. The biblical woman is shunned by her community because of the way they have labeled her. She is other, as are many other persons in present-day society, men and women, who are "shunned" in less obvious ways. The good news of the text is that Christ reaches out with new life to this woman and to the "other," regardless of how society has labeled them. Careful interpretation of scripture reveals that it is not God who presents a troublesome nature for human beings but rather the trouble lies with the interpretation, the redaction, the reading into the text a picture of God that does not represent the God of grace and love that offers good news to all people in all situations.

Good news preaching begins with the expectation of finding good news in the biblical text, and that good news is God, who in covenantal love extends care and concern for all of creation. Created male and female in the image of God, even from the biblical records that might offer a distorted picture, ours is a God of love who reaches out with unending grace to resolve the troubles that plague the hearts and lives of the people of God. The true picture of God, the God of scripture, is one of divine grace, covenantal love that prevails in all circumstances. Regardless of how troublesome the picture of God appears, the true revelation is the grace-full sovereign of unending love in creation, in the redemption of humanity, and as sustaining spirit.

THE SERMON

In the morning, when he returned to the city, he was hungry. And seeing a fig tree by the side of the road, he went to it and found nothing at all on it but leaves. Then he said to it, "May no fruit ever come from you again!" And the fig tree withered at once. When the disciples saw it, they were amazed, saying, "How did the fig tree wither at once?" Jesus answered them, "Truly I tell you, if you have faith and do not doubt, not only will you do what has been done to the fig tree, but even if you say to this mountain, 'Be lifted up and thrown into the sea,' it will be done. Whatever you ask for in prayer with faith, you will receive." (Matt. 21:18–22)

Have you ever noticed how some people's personality seems to change when they are hungry? Some people get cranky, some get irritable, some like my friend with low blood sugar get fussy and then pass out. Jesus seems to be part of the cranky group. Have you noticed? Think about it. Take the feeding of the five thousand. The disciples are observant—this time anyway—and they realize it's getting late and they are in an area where there's no place to buy food. Jesus is their leader, so they go to him. A nice quiet question, and he turns on them and says, "You give them something to eat." Then there's the time they are walking through the grain fields on the Sabbath. What does he do? Begins picking grain, and when the Pharisees, quite naturally, question him, he gives them a snappy answer—cranky! And that's probably what happened at the wedding when he snapped at his mother. He was probably hungry and waiting to be served—cranky! And for sure he's cranky after returning from spending the night at Bethany. He's hungry and he's cranky. Poor fig tree, confronted by a cranky Jesus. I don't know about you but that's not one of the characteristics I want my God to have. Who wants a cranky God? Next Jesus will start acting like the gods of the Romans and the Greeks and start killing off things he doesn't like. Wait! That's where we came in, isn't it? So what's this all about?

I remember this story as part of the Holy Week scriptures I heard as a child. It appears on the second day of Holy Week that commemorates Jesus' final days in Jerusalem. The Palm Sunday celebration of Jesus' entry into Jerusalem is over and the cleansing of the temple has been done. In righteous indignation he threw out the money changers who in the practice of their trade robbed those who could ill afford it, who had to buy animals for sacrifice and change their money into appropriate temple coins. No, that's not being cranky; that's just taking care of business, God's business.

Matthew records that Jesus left the people and went to Bethany and spent the night there. We are not given a specific location, but arriving hungry the next day most probably means that he was not at someone's home. He sees the fig tree; it has no figs and he uses his power to kill the tree. Why? This is a troublesome picture of Christ for me. The Jesus I know and love has time for children when adults, men, try to send them away. My Jesus allows women to be in his close company and even to touch him. He doesn't let temple rules stop him; no, he stops a crowd from stoning a woman, heals lepers, takes water from a Gentile woman, calms storms, restores sight, and I could go on and on. This Jesus who seems cranky and irritable does not fit the picture of the loving Savior that I hold in my heart . . . or does it? Again I ask, what's going on here?

The story appears between two visits that Jesus makes to the temple. The first is on the day that we celebrate as Palm Sunday, where Jesus makes his entry and is hailed as the coming King and then cleans the temple of defilers. The second has him facing the chief priests and the elders and defending his authority, or more correctly, being questioned about his authority. He doesn't waste time to defend it. Scholars consider the story of the fig tree to be a teaching moment for Jesus. It is a moment of instruction on faith shared with the disciples. He wants them to understand the power of faith and their ability, by faith, to do things that are out of the ordinary.

So why kill a perfectly good fig tree to make a point? Who says it was a perfectly good fig tree? It had no fruit, and Matthew's account, unlike Mark's gospel, does not say it was not fig-bearing time. The incident reminded me of being with my Dad in our garden and watching him cut down a banana tree. The tree seemed perfectly good to me so I asked my father why he cut down the tree. He explained that sometimes when a shoot comes out, although it grows well, it does not have the proper stuff that will allow it to bear fruit. But it grows anyway and takes nutrients from the soil that fruit-bearing trees need. So when that happens, you have to cut it down. Do you get it? When the tree will not bear fruit, it becomes a drain on the soil, a parasite if you will, and it must be removed.

That's the message, say the scholars. The fig tree is symbolic of Israel; and Jesus' action symbolizes God's judgment against Israel, which refuses to be nurtured in the Word of God and bear fruit. This seems to make sense because it is the message that the parables that follow in Matthew are all saying. Those who are not fruitful, who do not advance the reign of God on earth, are cut off.

And there's a second message for the disciples. Jesus says to them, just as I have been able to do extraordinary things, so too in my name will you do. It is a promise of power—the power of God to do miraculous things in the name of God, in the power of the living Christ. And we know that the disciples were able to perform miracles of healing and new life in the name of Jesus. But fast forward to us. What's the message for us in this strange text and from this troublesome Jesus?

We, the church, every Christian, we are all called to bear fruit in the name of Christ. We who have been nurtured on the word of God are not simply to stand by idling the time away, we are to do the things of Christ, we are to do that which strengthens our faith, and with that faith go out and do miracles in the name of Jesus Christ. Jesus himself said that his disciples would do greater things than he did. And he did some marvelous things, from giving new sight to the blind, putting lame people back on their feet, and even giving life to a man who was four days dead and buried.

And we can do the same in Jesus' name. Plenty of folk, even some in the church, are walking around blind to the blessings of God in their lives. By faith we can help them to see God in their midst. All around us in the world, people are crippled in mind and body and spirit because they have allowed the challenges of life to break them into little pieces. Through Christ they can be strengthened so that they can rise up and walk in newness of life, and we who live in that newness can show them the way. There are even people in our midst who are dead in their sins. They are walking around like zombies, dead inside, killed off in spirit by the troubles of the world. We have the power by faith to lead them to new life, to Christ, who is the way, the truth, the life. It's all a matter of faith.

That is what Jesus is saying to his disciples, saying to us. If you have faith there is nothing that will be too hard for you to accomplish. And I'm not talking about blind faith. Did not Jesus say if the blind leads the blind they will both end up in a ditch? No, I'm talking about living faith, open-your-eyes faith that can see the power of God at work in your own life and in the world. But there's another side to this message, one that each of us and the church need to take seriously.

If it is true, as Matthew and the interpreters say, that Jesus' action of cursing the fig tree, killing the fig tree, was a message to Israel about God's judgment toward "fruitless Judaism," as M. Eugene Boring names it in the *New Interpreter's Bible Commentary,* then what about a fruitless church? Could it be that there's a message, an urgent message here for us?

In my beloved United Methodist Church, we have been lamenting the continued loss of members and making doomsday predictions about the death of the denomination for years. The disciples questioned how the fig tree died so quickly, and if you listen to the pundits we are dying slowly. Or are we? Didn't I read somewhere that a thousand years are but a day in God's sight? So if we are dying it's happening pretty quickly, isn't it?

But we're not dead yet and Christ gives new life to the dying. Jesus Christ restores our life for living as kingdom dwellers. This cranky Jesus is hungry for the people who are called by his name to get up and begin to live their faith and do the things, bear the fruit that he has empowered us to do. This troublesome God is calling us to live into the faith and by the power of that faith that he has already given us. If we have faith and go forward in the strength of that faith, we will do miraculous things, things that are real and true; the things of God that Christ has directed and empowered us to do.

If we believe, when we believe, we will come to understand things as Christ gives us the power to understand; we will see as Christ sees, know as Christ knows, accept as Christ accepted his life, his death, and his resurrection. When we believe we open ourselves to receive by faith all that Christ has in store for us, and we can have all the life we need to bear all the fruit we must. When we believe we will even move mountains—mountains of doubt and fear—and we will kill trees—dead trees of apathy and unfaithfulness, trees whose fruits are lifelessness and emptiness.

Christ restores our faith and our life so that we can bear fruit in his name. Like Christ we may be hungry, but Christ knows our hunger and feeds us with the bread of heaven, feeds us with faith to go forward and, like trees planted by water and in good soil, bear fruit for him. Let us go forward nurturing our faith and living fruitful lives in the name of Jesus Christ, the pioneer and perfecter of our faith.

· 3 ·

IN THE FAMILY OF GOD

SIBLING RIVALRY OR PARENTAL PREFERENCE?

*As soon as Isaac had finished blessing Jacob, when Jacob had
scarcely gone out from the presence of his father Isaac, his brother
Esau came in from his hunting. He also prepared savory food, and
brought it to his father. And he said to his father, "Let my father
sit up and eat of his son's game, so that you may bless me." His
father Isaac said to him, "Who are you?" He answered, "I am your
firstborn son, Esau." Then Isaac trembled violently and said,
"Who was it then that hunted game and brought it to me, and I
ate it all before you came and I have blessed him?—yes, and
blessed he shall be!" (Gen. 27:30–33)*

I have always experienced a feeling of indignation at this part of
the Abrahamic saga. Somehow it has always seemed unfair that Jacob,
who stole his brother's birthright, should be the one through whom
the original covenant between God and Abraham should be realized.
In my experience, the stories of Jacob that I have heard most often

preached, in the effort to show God's constancy with the chosen ones, focus on either his dream at Bethel, where God renewed the covenant made to his ancestors, or his wrestling with the angel and the changing of his name from Jacob to Israel. Rarely, if ever, have I heard a message preached about the stealing of his brother's birthright. But then, neither have I heard particular focus given to the family system that is in operation in the household and the levels of dysfunction that cause trouble at multiple layers and on many occasions.

Jacob's perfidy is orchestrated by his mother, who is also Esau's mother and models for all time the calamity that arises from parents giving preferential treatment to one sibling over the others. Contrary to the prevailing belief, sibling rivalry was not the norm of the brothers' relationship, despite the report of Jacob holding on to Esau's heel at birth, and yet it becomes easy for Rebekah to conspire against her older son and for Jacob to agree to cheat his brother. What does it say about motherly love when it results in preferential treatment of one child over the other?

At its best the church is a loving family and it is made up of many families, loving and otherwise. In one local church that I served, I was advised by a very wise member to be very careful about speaking about any member to another because of the myriad family ties that existed in the church. It was not that I intended to indulge in such divisive behavior, but I appreciated her warning anyway. In that same church I discovered fraternal twins who did not speak to each other, although they and their families lived in the same house. And like the Jacob and Esau story, their disagreement stemmed from one sister's observation of their mother's favoritism of her sister.

Family systems are often dysfunctional. To my untutored eye it seems that one of the characteristics of family systems is a significant amount of dysfunction. I'm not sure that the experts in this area of study would agree, but still we have a biblical family that is recognized as God's chosen family through which the covenant will be fulfilled, and there is dysfunction everywhere. So how does this story give life to the people of God about what it means to be the family of God? Said another way, the question is, how does the preacher approach the task of preaching this text?

There is great difficulty in finding good news for preaching from this piece of the story. Most likely the preacher will read the full pericope of this part of the story that includes Esau begging for a blessing from his father only to hear that the ill done to him will be compounded and "By your sword you shall live, and you shall serve your brother; but when you break loose, you shall break his yoke from your neck" (Gen. 27:40). You can almost hear Esau say, "Whew! It will take work but at least I won't be under him forever. Still, my brother has to pay for stealing what was mine by right of my birth as the first-born son."

As in the congregation that I served, it is very likely that every congregation has some unhealthy family dynamics going on among the people. Thus in the analysis of the context the preacher is wise to include that possibility in order to determine how best to approach the text. Feelings of disillusionment, sadness, pain, and even abuse are common when there is betrayal of the love and support that family members expect from one another and consider the substance or the glue that keeps the family together. It may not be between siblings but between other close relatives or extended family members that the problem of a family at odds within the ranks causes tension that negatively affects each family member's ability to live into his or her full personhood and perhaps to receive the good news of God's equal and affirming love for all members of the family of God. In fact there is more to the biblical family story that may determine the preacher's approach in dealing with the many layers of trouble in this family and bringing alive the grace of God for the hearers.

When Esau was forty years old, he married Judith daughter of Beeri the Hittite, and Basemath daughter of Elon the Hittite; and they made life bitter for Isaac and Rebekah. (Gen. 26:34–35)

Although the placement of this snippet of family life comes before the deed perpetrated by Jacob in stealing his brother's birthright, it should in no way provide an excuse for the actions of his mother. It is, however, a reminder to us in this age of blended families and elder abuse of the part that religious beliefs may play in guiding a family and shaping its life together. When we bring others who hold different beliefs or cultural practices into an established family, the family dynamics are disturbed and changed and dysfunction may result. In the multicultural world of the twenty-first century, it is a consideration to be given to a preacher's approach to understanding the congregation.

The Hittites were Canaanites, not worshipers of the one true God, Yahweh, but that alone is not responsible for Basenath's behavior toward her in-laws. Certainly Isaac has been able to live peacefully with his foreign neighbors, but that same peace does not exist in his home. And perhaps it is this absence of peace that stirs Rebekah to take steps to ensure her comfort. What she orchestrates seems to have more to do with her own needs, given that, should Esau receive the birthright from his father, she will be totally subject to him as their culture and custom demands. And although the culture of society in the United States is not the same, in the midst of an economy that is causing parents and children to share the same living space as adults, the preacher must approach this text with new vision in order to respond with empowering good news in an ever-changing society.

Confronted only with the story of Jacob's perfidy, it is difficult to discern God's grace operating in the lives of this family in that particular moment, despite the promised blessing to Esau that one day he will come into his own. That is good news that speaks of resolution but not restitution. And that may be sufficient for the moment. Given the length and depth of the full story of this divinely chosen family, looking beyond this text and into the whole story is requisite in order to discern where God is at work transforming trouble for the good of the family. There is no easy answer to the problem of corrupt or dysfunctional family systems, and this story offers models for us of the unending grace of God that looks beyond faults and failures of individual lives and even of families to bring about the work of God in the world. That is good news worth preaching at all times. Beyond the particularities of the preaching context that determine the specifics of the sermon narrative, the story serves as a backdrop to the overarching story of the divine/human covenant, and it witnesses to the reality that God maintains an affirming relationship with those in the family of God, regardless of their misdeeds.

As Jacob's story continued and as the trickster met another of like mind in the person of his uncle Laban, one may wonder whether the behavior is simply a family pattern. But one wonders even more at the working of God's justice. God not only prospers Jacob but God redeems him so that he becomes the father of many nations. The family that seemed on the verge of mayhem, if not annihilation, as one brother plots to kill the other, is blessed by God as God keeps covenant, and the descendants of Abraham through Isaac are as numerous as God has promised. The story speaks to families in trouble. It is more than Isaac's or Jacob's or Esau's or Rebekah's story; it is a family story of the people of God, who overcome challenges to live according to the grace of God's enlivening presence. Thus it speaks to human families caught in the morass of unhealthy and perhaps destructive relationships with an assurance that God is able to bring about gracious resolution regardless of their situation. Nevertheless, it should not be used to justify maintaining unjust or destructive family relationships in the belief that God's grace will prevail. It is the responsibility of all people within or outside the family to seek justice for everyone.

FAMILY HONOR OR JUSTIFIED VIOLENCE?

Biblical history is replete with family stories that speak of trouble and grace in wide dimensions, and just as the ill treatment of a mother may have incited her to take action against family members, so too does action perpetrated against a sister cause brothers to take murderous action against the abuser. In the same way that family stories can be traced throughout the Hebrew scriptures, so too can the stories of abuse and neglect of women. Many of these stories are not given the light of day and most of these often gruesome texts are left out of lectionary charts. Even among preachers who are not bound to preselected scriptures, the challenge of dealing with such stories is more than the average preacher wants to engage. It is easier to skirt around issues of abuse and revenge and family dynamics that turn deadly.

Now Dinah the daughter of Leah, whom she had borne to Jacob, went out to visit the women of the region. When Shechem son of

Hamor the Hivite, prince of the region, saw her, he seized her and lay with her by force. And his soul was drawn to Dinah daughter of Jacob; he loved the girl and spoke tenderly to her. So Shechem spoke to his father Hamor saying, "Get me this girl to be my wife." (Gen. 34:1–4)

Scholars have argued whether or not rape, in the sense that it is understood generally, did occur. All agree, however, that there was a violent sexual encounter. Frank Yamada notes:

The key issue that defines the violation for most interpreters is female violation or consent. In other words rape is defined as an act of sexual violation and aggression against the will of another person. However, the problem with such a definition within the context of Genesis 34 is that Dinah never speaks.[1]

Statistics on rape victims report that one in six women has been the victim of sexual abuse and 60 percent of victims do not report the abuse.[2] These women do not speak. Like Dinah they remain voiceless perhaps in fear of the stigma that will be placed on them, even in today's society. Given those statistics, it is likely that there are such women in every congregation, and the biblical stories of abuse may cause them to replay their own experience in their minds. Many women not only do not report the violation of their person to the authorities, they also do not discuss what has occurred with family members due to the feelings of shame they suffer despite the fact that they were not responsible for their victimization.

Yamada's observation regarding the text and Dinah's voicelessness is significant. "Dinah does not cry out; in fact she does not say anything throughout the whole narrative. The narrator's focus is on the actions and responses of men; hence the reader has no way of knowing Dinah's response."[3] Her brothers, in the name of family honor, plot and ultimately kill all the men of Shechem's society. The men have taken the attack on their sister as an attack on the family. Their actions of revenge are aimed at satisfying family honor, and, since Dinah's voice is never heard, one wonders at her feelings regarding her birth family in light of the new family that she is about to have. From the biblical record there is evidence that she has begun to be part of a new family. According to the text she is already in Shechem's house when her brothers do their dastardly deed.

> *They killed Hamor and his son Shechem with the sword, and took Dinah out of Shechem's house, and went away. (Gen. 34:26)*

The family that has settled in a new place, Jacob's family, and the family that has begun to be created by Dinah and Shechem are both disrupted. The first is uprooted and must seek a new location, the second is uprooted before it is fully planted and dies. In fact death is all around, in murdered lives and killed hopes and dreams. Where is God in all this? What is the good news for families in our time when so much of society is plagued by violence?

The preacher who is daring enough to take on this text—and hopefully some preachers are, especially in the light of the continued violence against women through rape and other forms of abuse, both physical and emotional, and the prevalence of murders in many communities where entire families are killed—must resist the temptation to justify any of the abusive action that ensues. Shechem's abuse of Dinah is unacceptable in any form, even if he later decides to marry her. Marriage does not guarantee that there will not be further violence done to her person; statistics show that domestic violence too often escalates to the point of murder.[4] But the family systems that support both Shechem and Dinah are worthy of note.

As custom decrees, Shechem goes to his father to have the marriage arranged. Although Jacob and his family are foreigners, Hamor supports his son and arranges to add a new daughter, Dinah, into his household. Likewise, Dinah is supported by her family. They are justly upset by Shechem's original treatment of their sister, but as is customary, the woman is not allowed to make her wishes known. On pretense of inviting the outsiders into the wider family, the brothers perpetrate an act of vengeance that is so far outside the range of normalcy that it disrupts the entire family. The trouble brought upon the men of the city is as heinous as some of the violence perpetrated today by drug lords, and it is all done in the name of family honor.

How is this act by members of the chosen family of God instructive for preaching, and where is there good news to be found? Additionally, there are cultural implications interwoven with the family dynamics. Dinah is Israelite and Shechem is Hivite. Perhaps it is easier for Dinah's brothers to kill Shechem because he is not part of the wider Israelite family.

Given the prevalence of violence in the world, it is likely that there will be those in the congregation who see this story as support for their own feelings of vengeance against any who might have done wrong to members of their family. The text offers a warning that violence begets greater violence and does more to disrupt lives that it does to bring about retribution for the harm one has suffered. The story of dysfunction in the family does not end with violence against the outsider; it is these same brothers who later plot to do violence against their brother Joseph. It is unlikely that the situation recorded in this text will be an actual picture of a present situation, but the prevalence for violence in the world opens the possibility that whole families can be wiped out by the need for revenge at an actual or perceived slight. In this story, God's supporting presence for Jacob and his descendents guides him to the next stage of the journey. Thus, as before, the good news is that God does not abandon us in the midst of the trials of life. That does not mean that any of us is free to perpetrate violence of body or spirit against anyone for the sake of the family. Whatever our individual human families, whatever the culture to which we belong, we are all part of the family of God.

TO THE THIRD AND FOURTH GENERATION

Many Christian preachers bypass the stories of the Hebrew scriptures in the mistaken belief that not only are they not relevant to the present, but also the God of the Hebrew Bible is different in nature and purpose than the God of the New Testament or of the present. As such, when the sermon is based on a Hebrew Bible text, these preachers consider it necessary, if not essential, that the sermon move beyond the particular historical period in which it is situated and into the New Testament, in order to find evidence that they consider relevant and significant in affirming God's faithfulness to the present congregation.

Although the Hebrew Bible stories themselves require an appropriate interpretive lens, the same is true of the entire biblical record.

For preachers who claim a Judeo-Christian heritage, the Hebrew records also shine brightly with the light of God's redemptive grace offered constantly and consistently to people and systems mired in sin. Within the stories of kings and prophets and ordinary people are today's stories under different covers and called by different names. Adultery is still a major cause of brokenness and sin in families and in society. Although reported through different media, the notoriety experienced by persons in power or those whose fame is a by-product of their life's work is similar to that of the rich and famous of Bible times. TV programs remind us that murder is still considered a way out when the situation is beyond someone's control.

> *It happened, late one afternoon, when David rose from his couch and was walking about on the roof of the king's house, that he saw from the roof a woman bathing; the woman was very beautiful. David sent someone to inquire about the woman. It was reported, "This is Bathsheba daughter of Eliam, the wife of Uriah the Hittite." So David sent messengers to get her, and she came to him, and he lay with her. (Now she was purifying herself after her period.) Then she returned to her house. The woman conceived; and she sent and told David, "I am pregnant." (2 Sam. 11:2–5)*

This story is entitled in most Bibles that use titular headings as David's adultery. And so it is. But it is rarely, if ever, called the rape of Bathsheba. Reading it, I have again and again been filled with a sense of dis-ease at the injustice done to this woman both by King David and then by the writers of history.

Adultery implies consent on the part of all parties concerned, but in the case of Bathsheba she is the victim of rape at the hands of the one who is the head of the greater family of Israel. In one moment she is ripped from the moorings of her home and family and is soon to be a widow. The resulting pregnancy, usually a time of joy and celebration for a woman of her culture, brings further shame and anguish as she must report her condition to her abuser. She must, because she has nowhere else to turn. Should her husband learn of it he will denounce her as an adulterer and she will be stoned to death. It is the end of the hopes and dreams of her life with Uriah. And even as the king tries to make things right, hoping that Uriah will make it easy for the problem to go away, she knows that if he does she will be forced to live a lie. And finally she is made to suffer in sorrow at the death of her husband and then the death of her child. So where is the good news in Bathsheba's story? It seems like there is only trouble beyond the trouble one expects in everyday life.

Viewed from a distance, it is as though the judgment of God has fallen on her, as though she has become the scapegoat for the sin done to her family. In a similar yet different way, it compares to the situation faced by too many young women who are abused or engage in semiconsensual sexual encounters that are basically forced upon them because of the power deferential between the women and their partners, only to suffer the consequence not only of unexpected and unwanted pregnancies but also of the death of their own and their family's dreams. In many cases the disruption to the family is widespread and far-reaching. In some areas of society it has reached epidemic proportions, with girls finding their futures placed on hold and families forced to realign themselves around the needs of mother and child. Often young women have no one to turn to and no one with whom to find refuge. Without family support they become victims of a society overburdened by the need to be family to these children in unprecedented and overwhelming ways.

Society does not constitute family, and its systems cannot provide the familial support that is needed in such circumstances. Preaching this text without moving too quickly through the trauma suffered by the sexual violence perpetrated by one man opens the door for the preacher to offer the hearers an affirming word of the omnipresence of God's love regardless of the overshadowing caused by the aberrant behavior of the people involved. It calls for a living witness of the divine presence in the lives of the people, gathered for worship, who must live into their role as the family of God. As family, they provide support and protection in the name of the One who is the head over all the families on earth. It is grace incarnate that mitigates the trouble of the situation.

The power dynamics of family systems can create safe space in which to experience God's abiding presence and they can also bring about disastrous consequences when they are allowed to overwhelm those who are part of the system.

> *So Tamar took the cakes she had made, and brought them into the chamber to Amnon her brother. But when she brought them near to him to eat, he took hold of her, and said to her, "Come, lie with me, my sister." She answered him, "No, my brother, do not force me, for such a thing is not done in Israel; do not do anything so vile! As for me, where could I carry my shame? And as for you, you would be as one of the scoundrels in Israel. Now, therefore, I beg you, speak to the king; for he will not withhold me from you." But he would not listen to her; and being stronger than she, he forced her and lay with her. (2 Sam. 13:10c–14)*

Children learn from their parents. Amnon has learned from his father, David, that he can take anything he wants. David and Bathsheba's connection is no longer a secret, and Amnon follows the violent trail left by his father by tricking his half sister and violently raping her.

Incest has become a visible plague in today's society. Brothers are raping sisters, fathers are raping daughters, and mothers are even raping sons, not to mention the extended family—aunts and uncles and grandparents—who are taking advantage of weak and helpless children and young people. It is a breakdown of the family in extreme proportions. The damage done to the victims is catastrophic, and the damage done to the family cannot be calculated. What is worse is that many persons who are victimized as children or young people become perpetrators of the same abuse that they suffered. Across all levels of society, the trauma suffered by victims and the loss of self they experience is evidenced in this story. It offers a way of connecting especially with those, like Tamar and Bathsheba, who are made voiceless and have no say in the retributive justice that is theirs by right. Yamada contends, "The rape acts as an important catalyst for the issue of family rivalry and succession that result. It is the first link in a whole chain of events that works toward the fulfillment of Yahweh's word against David."[5]

There is often silence when the situation of abuse, particularly sexual abuse, is a feature of family life. There is shame on the part of the victim, who often feels as though she or he is the cause of the brokenness that has infected the family. The victim often remains silent in fear that speaking out will totally shatter the family and it will disappear. Victims remain silent because, as broken as the family is, the need for family of any kind is great. When that happens, the loss of self is suffered in way that is often irretrievable. This story in Tamar and other texts like these speak of deep trouble and thus need an outpouring of grace to balance the scale and bring light to the deep darkness that they represent.

The preacher can allow the text to speak in its own words only when the offering of grace overflows and covers the devastation of injury that the text details. Preaching good news in a sermon that deals with such brokenness is essential and must be offered with the same care that one would give to an actual victim. Who knows whether there is a real victim present? The good news must help to give voice to the silenced, open ears that can hear silent screams, and open eyes to see into the hearts of those in pain. It is a tall order for the preacher, but to sidestep this text in today's society is to miss an opportunity to help restore life through the offering of divine love.

In order to find good news for preaching, beyond the normative assurance of God's presence with the victim in times of trouble, the preacher is forced to move beyond the text and into the wider story of God's redemption of the family. This does not mean going to God's ultimate act of redemption in Jesus Christ; rather, what it requires is the recognition of God's saving grace toward David and even to the offspring of David and Bathsheba, King Solomon, who earns the title of the greatest king of Israel. It is a long journey on which to take the congregation, but the evidence of God's perseverance to redeem this family that is so bound up in sin is a worthy endeavor to offer reassurance to present-day families that God is indeed aware of the darkness of their plight and is present to bring them out into the light of God's glory. The extravagance of God's love extends beyond the sinful actions done to us or even by us so that restoration and wholeness is guaranteed through the grace of God.

FOR LOVE OF THE CHILD

Now his elder son was in the field; and when he came and approached the house, he heard music and dancing. He called one of the slaves and asked what was going on. He replied, "Your brother has come, and your father has killed the fatted calf because he has got him back safe and sound." Then he became angry and refused to go in. His father came out and began to plead with him. But he answered his father, "Listen! For all these years I have been working like a slave for you, and I have never disobeyed your command; yet you have never given me even a young goat so that I might celebrate with my friends. But when this son of yours came back, who has devoured your property with prostitutes, you killed the fatted calf for him!" (Luke 15:25–30)

Sounds like jealousy or perhaps sibling rivalry or even favoritism on the part of the father, doesn't it? When taken out of the context of the complete story that is called the parable of the prodigal son, these six verses may bring to mind a different image than that of the overly generous and forgiving father. In fact, some refer to this story as the parable of the prodigal father, given that one of the meanings of the word prodigal is "recklessly extravagant."[6] But when we look at the events from the perspective of family systems and the implied message of this story to persons who are caught in unhealthy and even abusive family relations, the widely preached interpretation that lauds the actions of the father may not offer such good news, as the father's benevolence to his younger son implies, to the mistreated, bypassed, or ignored sibling sitting in the congregation.

As in the Bible, so it is in both movies and in myriad real-life situations today—emotional abuse caused by blatant favoritism on the part of parents has caused sibling rivalry that has resulted in violence of body and spirit, including murder. An interpretation of the historical culture of this text shows that the action of the younger son in asking for his inheritance prior to his father's death was tantamount to killing his father or saying simply, "I wish you were dead." Despite this, the father accedes to his son's request, liquidates the assets necessary, and sends the younger son off, if not with his blessing, certainly with some kind of approbation. R. Allen Culpepper, New Testament scholar, asserts that while the perceived favoritism of the younger son is contrary to normal culture and tradition, it seems to fit a biblical pattern wherein "the younger son is favored in the stories of Israel's heritage."[7] Certainly it is the older son, the firstborn, who is entitled by tradition to the major share of his father's wealth. The older son knows this, and seeing his father give the portion (and we do not know exactly how much that was) to his brother may already have caused this older brother, the heir apparent, to wonder whether it depleted the amount that would come to him.

I have heard many preachers, and I have even preached this way, tell about the father's great love that caused him not only to keep looking in the distance for his lost son, but also, on seeing the son from a long way off, to forget about the dignity that was expected of him and run to meet his son. It is truly a demonstration of a father's great love for even a wayward child. And that is good news for anyone who has wandered away from God and is desirous of finding the way back into right relationship with God. That God's heart is always open is a message of divine grace that must be preached often to the people of God. But what about the older son, the child who feels neglected and taken for granted, whose experience is of a parent who longs for a sibling who has abandoned home and said parent, yet who remains at the center of that parent's heart?

It is the experience of too many children, both young and of adult age, that one or both parents show a distinct attitude of favoritism. Also too often the sibling who remains at home to care for incapacitated or aging parents or who sacrifices his or her own life dreams is unappreciated at best, sometimes even abused emotionally by the ones for whom he or she has become the major caregiver. Although this is not the situation in Jesus' parable, a sermon preached on this text that commends the father for his abounding, forgiving love or, worse yet, condemns the older son for having a jealous or unforgiving attitude may cause an underappreciated or abused caregiver sitting in the pews to experience even further hurt. Given the necessity for the care of elderly parents that many of today's families face, it is almost certain that such a situation is represented in the congregation, compounding the challenges of preaching this parable.

Once again the preacher is confronted by a text whose good news presents difficulties for certain persons or groups in the congregation. Even the father's response does not help to relieve the situation or that elder son's feeling of hurt. Yet it is important that the older brother's hurt is treated with the same grace that the younger wastrel son receives.

> *Son, you are always with me, and all that is mine is yours. But we had to celebrate and rejoice, because this brother of yours was dead and has come to life; he was lost and has been found. (Luke 15:31b–32)*

Why? asks the older brother in his heart. What is there to celebrate? Who says that he will not take you for all he can and run off again? The father's words seem to reinforce the older son's feeling of being taken for granted. He knows that as the heir he will receive the total of his father's estate, but that is in the future. This is now and to his mind his brother does not deserve any share of all that he has helped to build up while his brother was away enjoying himself. Scholars point out the fact that at the opening of the parable it speaks about "sons" but here at the end of the story the term is "brothers," which identifies and claims the familial relationship between the sons. It may well be perceived that the change of term is meant to underscore the fact that there is a relationship between the two that is separate from that which is connected to their father.

The younger brother has indulged his vices fully before returning home. In today's society, one of the unfortunate realities in families is the issue of drug abuse. Family members who abuse legal or illegal drugs are quickly ruled by their addiction and will do and say anything to feed their addiction. Often the result is abuse of family members, and the entire family system is negatively affected, as there is division along the line of how and whether to continue to receive the offender into the bosom of the family. This story may touch the heart of family members who are suffering through the agony of losing a member to the drugs or to other street vices again and again. It may resound with hope that one so lost will return or with hopelessness that the member may return yet again and the joy of the return will be clouded by the recollection of other returns to home and then back to the vice of choice. The older brother's resentment may strike a sharp chord in the heart of individuals or the entire family, and they need to hear a word of grace as they try to be a family bound by love.

Jesus' purpose for telling parables is to teach his followers about the family of God, God's realm, so it is appropriate that his teaching should provide guidance for the familial relationships of all the people of God. Preaching beyond this difficulty means reframing the language of the text in the context of the unbounded, expansive, and eternal love of God. Naming God as the prodigal father with unlimited capacity and unfettered love for all people becomes crucial to preaching beyond the difficulty and to offering good news to the hearers. Such a presentation brings to light the love that is the necessary center of all families. Preaching the good news of this story means bringing into play all the nuances of human trouble evidenced by both sons and even by a father who seems to prefer one son over the other. It means allowing the grace of God to refocus the hearers' attention so that each can recognize her or his place in each character and ultimately receive the mitigating grace of God for her or his own life. At some time each of us may be the father, the older son, or the younger son. For the moment of the sermon we each find our place in the story based on our place in life, but whoever we are, it is a family portrait that invites each person to be the recipient of God's saving love.

Other family situations in scripture invite our attention as we strive to live not only as individual witnesses of Christ but also as the family of Christ. There were several pairs of brothers among Jesus' disciples, James and John, Simon and Andrew, and James and Matthew the sons of Alphaeus. But among the female followers there was also the mother of James and John, and her concern for her children's welfare took on dimensions that were troubling to the rest of the disciples—the rest of the family, so to speak.

Then the mother of Zebedee's sons came to Jesus with her sons and, kneeling down, asked a favor of him. "What is it you want?" he asked. She said, "Grant that one of these two sons of mine may sit at your right and the other at your left in your kingdom." (Matt. 20:20–21 NIV)

It was a bold, audacious request. Mark's gospel has the brothers making this request of Jesus on their own (Mark 10:35–37), but in Matthew it's a family affair. After all, isn't that what a mother is supposed to do? Doesn't every mother want the best for her children? All this mother is doing is looking out for her sons, seeking their interest, trying to make sure that their place in Christ's realm is assured.

Unfortunately in society, today's as well as across time, there have been mothers who are so caught up in making sure that their children are well taken care of that they have committed crimes and done awful deeds for the benefit of their children. On a much lesser scale mothers and fathers take on roles that set poor examples for their children's ethical and spiritual development. Take for example the mother who took on the role of bullying one of her daughter's friends, or the father who attacked the children on the school bus who were bullying his disabled daughter. And then there are the soccer and softball and Little League moms and dads whose behavior has even gotten some of them banned from attending their children's games.

Jesus quickly disabused this mother of the notion that her sons deserved any special privilege, but how can this text be heard by parents who see their role as that of perpetual protector of their children, regardless of their age? Scholars do not give much attention to the familial elements of mother and sons, but hearers may well focus on this element of the story. Untutored in biblical hermeneutics as much of the congregation is, some might miss the nuances of Jesus' response that offers good news to all hearers. Regardless of our earthly family, we are all part of the family of God. The care of our earthly family is only part of the responsibility of each person to live fully as part of God's family. Thus our actions, whether in support of family members or not, identify our true affiliation with the family of God as they redound to the greater good of all people. Additionally, God is the one who determines the placement of family members at the divine table. The other disciples objected to the request of this mother because it represented preferential treatment. Jesus' response reminds us that God gives equal treatment and attention to everyone and through Christ models for us the ideal of family life wherein all are treated with equal love and attention.

A PLACE IN THE FAMILY

As Jesus implied, anyone may be seated at the right or left hand of God. That is good news that followers of Christ need to hear. Christians today need that good news of a place prepared for those who do the will of God. Not only that, but Jesus offers the assurance that God has indeed prepared such a place of prestige for members of the family of God. And since Jesus has called his disciples to set aside their natural family in the interest of advancing the family of God, the assurance of a prepared place and recognition by God was a critical message for their time and perhaps even for ours.

> *"Do not think that I have come to bring peace to the earth; I have not come to bring peace, but a sword. For I have come to set a man against his father, and a daughter against her mother, and a daughter-in-law against her mother-in-law; and one's foes will be members of one's own household. Whoever loves father or mother more than me is not worthy of me; and whoever loves son or daughter more than me is not worthy of me. . . ." (Matt. 10:34–37)*

These are difficult words for Jesus' time, for Matthew's time, and for our time. Biblical scholars believe that this teaching was representative of a real situation in Matthew's church where newly converted Christians were forced to make the difficult choice between their family and their newfound faith. In fact there are still places in the world where Christians are persecuted for their faith and at times it is the members of their family who betray them to the authorities. Even in the United States there are family members that separate themselves from others in the family because of religious beliefs, both within and outside the Christian faith.

Most of us are not faced with the choice of following Christ or being alienated from our families, but as part of the greater family of the community, the society, or even the world, living according to

Christian principles sometimes puts us at odds with those who have differing beliefs and lifestyles. Even within natural families there are times when one is called to stand against ideas or activities that are contrary to Christian teachings. There are also so-called Christian sects that teach and follow doctrines that are oppressive and unjust. The remainder of this text reinforces Jesus' call for separation from that which would stand in the way of serving God faithfully. Matthew's text underscores his belief in the Christian family, the family of God. One's natural family is subject to the greater family that exists as the body of Christ. That is the intrinsic message of this text, but it does not translate well into today's church where divisions of race and class and doctrine separate the family of God, and where those who believe that theirs is the only right way to worship adopt a silo mentality, which excludes any and all who do not share their particular beliefs.

And yet Jesus is still the head of the church. Our allegiance is still, above all, to Christ. The expansive, all-inclusive teaching of Christ guides us and makes the difference in our understanding of the family of God. The good news of this text is that we are all members of the family of God and thus we are embraced in the divine love of our heavenly parent so that we can embrace others with that love. As the text unfolds, Christ speaks of the necessity to reach out with arms of love to those in need, to embrace those whom the world rejects, to speak for those who have been silenced, and to lift up those who have been downtrodden. In other words Christ invites us to be family to others even as we experience the love of God through our membership in the family of God.

Being family means reaching out and embracing those who are in need. God has already reached out to us through Jesus Christ; that is the assurance that we have through the death and resurrection of Jesus Christ. When difficult times come and life seems overwhelming, the family of God is the place and the persons to whom we can turn. It is not infeasible that Jesus might have been influenced by his mother's story and the support given by family members in her time of need.

In those days Mary set out and went with haste to a Judean town in the hill country, where she entered the house of

Zechariah and greeted Elizabeth. When Elizabeth heard Mary's greeting, the child leaped in her womb. And Elizabeth was filled with the Holy Spirit and exclaimed with a loud cry, "Blessed are you among women and blessed is the fruit of your womb. And why has this happened to me, that the mother of my Lord comes to me? For as soon as I heard the sound of your greeting, the child in my womb leaped for joy. And blessed is she who believed that there would be a fulfillment of what was spoken to her by the Lord." (Luke 1:39–45)

In the movie *Quinceañera*, a young Mexican girl, about to turn fifteen, becomes pregnant. She has not had sexual intercourse and no one believes her. Her father, a pastor, feels shame because of her condition and forces her to leave the house. She moves in with her great-uncle who is already sheltering a male cousin who has been forced to leave his parents' home because of his homosexuality. It is a family story. Mary's travel to her cousin Elizabeth at the start of her pregnancy is also a family story. The text does not tell us that she is forced to leave her home, but until the angel speaks to Joseph she is at risk of losing her betrothed, her family, and even her life. She can be stoned for adultery. So to that extent there is pressure for her to do something to protect herself and her status in the family.

Although in today's society there is not the same stigma attached to pregnancy that occurs out of wedlock, in many ways there is a subtler stoning that takes place in the church and in society. In the Methodist Church in which I grew up, and in fact in all the mainline churches of my birth country, a baby born out of wedlock could not be baptized as part of the regular Sunday worship service. There was a weekday service where the child was baptized with only the parents and godparents of the child present. Perhaps it was thought that the sight of the child would corrupt the minds of the remaining virgin girls. Children born out of wedlock were such a disgrace that girls who found themselves in such a condition sought instead to abort the fetus in any way possible. The result was often death from botched abortions. At other times, women claimed the parentage of their unwed daughter's baby and the child was raised as sibling to its mother. In other cases, similar to Mary's story, the pregnant young woman was sent to live with relatives in the (far) country. Children are God's gift to us and they are meant to be a source of good news, but they are not considered such when young mothers and fathers cannot but see their lives change in ways that are overwhelming and, in their minds, destructive.

The text of Mary's pregnancy by the Holy Spirit and her travel to Elizabeth for support is not usually considered difficult. As part of the Christmas story, it is a joyful reenactment of the greatest story ever told. God incarnate, Christ come to earth, the Savior of the world conceived, if not yet born. For the young woman sitting in the pew who has yet to work up the nerve to tell her parents, hearing the story is agony. It is a painful reminder of the trouble in which she finds herself. Perhaps she wonders where she can go. Where is her hill country? Who is her Elizabeth? Where is the family that will comfort her and support her during her time of confinement? If she has admitted her condition and sought societal help, the check that she receives from governmental sources provides minimum support for her needs and that of her child, but not enough to allow her to escape her circumstances and improve her situation in a significant way. In fact, it often becomes a trap that compounds her life problems because it is just enough and too little at the same time.

Preaching good news from this text is easy because we know the end of the story, and certainly this part has a very happy ending with angels singing and shepherds rejoicing. Not so the story of today's pregnant teenager. She knows only that it is the end of her dreams and it is the end of life as she knows it, and she needs a word of hope that will ensure her that God is with her to bring her through the trouble. More than that, she needs the assurance of her second family, the church, that their support is real, that like the head, Christ, who stands with her, the body, Christ's body, is physically and spiritually by her side walking with her out of trouble through the grace of God.

It is unusual that preachers would think that Mary's story of immaculate conception could serve any purpose other than to celebrate the coming of the Christ child, but we live in a world of such complexity that preachers cannot search too deeply into scripture in order to allow it, at every moment of preaching, to speak to the realities of life. The church is representative of the family of God, or it must be. It cannot allow the dysfunction that is a part of so many natural families, and which they bring with them into the church, to misshape the family of God. The church itself is a family system and models for the natural families how the love of God that binds the members together works for the good of the whole family. When the church absconds from its responsibility, members are hurt and the lives of church families are disrupted. God with us guides the family in ways of love.

The good news of Immanuel, God with us, is not simply the power of Christ in the world. It is the presence of Christ through us to the world and to all those who are part of our world and therefore family members through Christ. Regardless of the text, the good news must always be relevant to the context in which it is preached. Thus, although suggestions were made as specific texts were addressed, the content of the good news must fit the people to whom it is delivered. The families to whom the message is delivered must be able to picture themselves within the images provided by the sermon. Through Christ, we are one family and, with him as head, the difficulties of life revealed through the biblical texts can find relief as the preacher offers the good news of God's eternal grace extended freely to all, for we are all members of the family of God.

THE SERMON

After two full years Absalom had sheepshearers at Baal-hazor, which is near Ephraim, and Absalom invited all the king's sons. Absalom came to the king, and said, "Your servant has sheepshearers; will the king and his servants please go with your servant?" But the king said to Absalom, "No, my son, let us not all go, or else we will be burdensome to you." He pressed him, but he would not go but gave him his blessing. Then Absalom said, "If not, please let my brother Amnon go with us." The king said to him, "Why should he go with you?" But Absalom pressed him until he let Amnon and all the king's sons go with him. Absalom made a feast like a king's feast. Then Absalom commanded his servants, "Watch when Amnon's heart is merry with wine, and when I say to you, 'Strike Amnon,' then kill him. Do not be afraid; have I not myself commanded you? Be courageous and valiant." So the servants of Absalom did to Amnon as Absalom had commanded. Then all the king's sons rose, and each mounted his mule and fled. . . .

So Absalom lived two full years in Jerusalem without coming into the king's presence. Then Absalom sent for Joab to send him to the king; . . . Then Joab went to the king and told him; and he summoned Absalom. So he came to the king and prostrated himself with his face to the ground before the king; and the king kissed Absalom. (2 Sam. 13:23–29, 14:28, 33)

In the movie *The Godfather II,* Michael Corleone, who has inherited the family business and the title of Godfather from his father, has an attempt made on his life. He leaves his home and travels to Cuba to be part of a multimillion dollar deal related to development in Cuba. While he is there the rebels overthrow the government, the deal is cancelled, and he is forced to flee, but more devastating is the knowledge he gains there that his brother Fredo was part of the conspiracy to assassinate him. Earlier in the story he had warned Fredo never to take anyone's side against the family. This new knowledge is more than he can bear and he determines that his brother must be killed, but he bides his time.

Absalom has been biding his time. His half brother Amnon had raped his sister. Tamar is half sister to Amnon but full sister to Absalom, and Absalom is livid. But he is biding his time. Their father has been told of the violation of his daughter, but King David does nothing to his firstborn. Perhaps he realizes that his son's actions are related to his own. Not long before, he had used his power as king to commandeer his wife Bathsheba, at that time the wife of Uriah, commander of his army, and he had lain with her against her will. Perhaps he considers how he had Uriah massacred when he could not get him to have sex with his wife so they could pass the child off as Uriah's. Perhaps it is simply that his love for his son causes him to turn a blind eye to Amnon's perfidy. Whatever the reason, David does nothing, and Absalom is biding his time.

David is the king of Israel. He was chosen by God and anointed by Samuel in the name of Yahweh. He is the keeper of justice, but he does nothing. He hears Absalom's complaint and he refuses to act against his favorite son, Amnon. It's a family matter and David as the head of both the natural family and of God's chosen family refuses to uphold the law of God. Where's the justice? Where's the familial care, even for a daughter? Does he even care about what this is doing to his family? David is silent in the face of the serious injustice perpetrated against his daughter by his son.

Tamar on the other hand is taken completely out of the loop. She had tried to prevent the rape. She had pleaded with her brother to seek legal means instead of force if he wanted her, but not only would he not agree, after the rape he hated her with the same intensity that he had desired her before he violated her. The Deuteronomic law (22:28–29) decrees that "if a man meets a virgin who is not engaged and seizes her and lies with her, and they are caught in the act, the man . . . must pay the young woman's father, . . . and she shall become his wife" for life, with no possibility of divorce. But Tamar is violated, raped violently, and left to suffer her shame in silence. Like so many women who are violated by family members, friends, dates, or people that they know, she feels helpless and maybe even hopeless. What future is there for her when her situation becomes known? How has such violation changed the lives of the many women who suffer in silence? Has the forced silence damaged their souls?

Her brother Absalom is also silent in the face of his father's inaction at the heinous deed. But it has damaged his soul. All he can think about is revenge. If his father won't give him justice, then he, Absalom, will execute vengeance on his brother. And for two full years Absalom waits, all the time holding on to his anger, allowing it to fester in his soul as he plots to kill his brother. It is the sad result of all who take upon themselves the role of God. Our task is to seek justice. God alone executes judgment and takes vengeance.

On the surface everything in the family seems okay, but underneath there is continued pain and agony experienced by Tamar, whose voice is missing, and by Absalom, who plots quietly until the right day comes. In so many of our families there are hidden hurts, hidden pain, sadness, and sorrow that are submerged beneath smiling faces. When life in community, in our families at home and in the church, is not representative of the love and justice that witnesses to the presence of God, then there is no true peace for those who are part of the family.

The sheep-shearers festival and celebration give Absalom the opportunity he has been waiting for. He sends a special invitation to his brother and, despite initial misgivings, David allows Amnon to attend. But Absalom cannot do the deed himself. In a pattern resembling his father's murder of Uriah, he orders his servants to kill a drunken Amnon and then he runs off to remain in hiding for the next three years.

It's a Mafia story isn't it? Ah, but it isn't, not really. Or maybe it is because the Mafia also consider themselves a family. It's a family story. Do you see it? It's all about family systems and the way they operate—pitting one side, one person, against the other. It's a dysfunctional family system that enables a pattern of violence to continue from person to person, across generations. It's reflective of many of our own families. Oh we're not all about to kill each other physically, but words have power to kill the soul. And because we allow our souls to be infected by silent anger and unrelieved pain, we respond with violent words that are sharper than the proverbial sword. We stab each other in the places where we hurt the most, where no one on the outside sees, in the midst of family and laughter and celebrations and then we run away to hide from God because of the shame and the fear that follows our destructive deeds.

Although I teach my students to beware of the ubiquitous "we," I've been saying we because there is so much violence in many of our family systems today that, even if we have the best and most functional family in the world, chances are that we all know of at least one dysfunctional family. And if the biblical story seems somewhat extreme, I must tell you that unfortunately, even today, there are families in which rape and incest is a daily nightmare to some young girl or boy who feels powerless and remains silent because he or she feels no one is listening, no one will hear. Not only that, but because the need to be part of a family is so intrinsic to who we are as human beings, victims of all ages remain silent because the thought of tearing the family apart, as the child knows will be the result if she or he speaks out, is too heavy a burden to bear. So they remain silent, becoming truly voiceless, hoping against hope that their silent screams will yet break through the wall of protective silence that surrounds the family and they will be rescued. There are patterns of physical violence in families where children and the elderly have their souls killed daily in the blows that are inflicted on their tired, pain-ridden bodies. And perpetrators, who may have once been beaten in the same way, cannot stop. With every blow they strike they remember the feeling on their own bodies and suffer the repeated death of their own souls, but they cannot stop.

Absalom hid from his father for three years and then he sought an intermediary to reach out to his father for forgiveness. Joab had already found a way to get David to face his own wrongdoing, so David had already begun the work of reclaiming his soul and reuniting his family. It took someone outside the immediate family to bring the two together, to bring Absalom back into his father's life. And it worked. And David and Absalom met face to face and David forgave Absalom and they lived happily ever after.

Not so quick, my friends. If you know the whole story you know that this is not the end. There is more mayhem and madness to come, but stop here with me for this time. Let's look again at what it took to bring at least these members of the family together. It took someone who was committed to the cause of family unity, perhaps even of bringing love back to the hearts of those who had been estranged. Amnon is still dead, but there is great opportunity for forgiveness and peace.

It is the same in our family systems. When we have been wronged, once the wrong has been done there is little that can be done to bring things back to the way they were before the trouble started. The ultimate is justice for the victim and at times even that is not possible. There was no justice for Tamar. We don't hear about her life from this point on. It is almost as though she is a pawn in some bizarre male family game. But thanks be to God, that does not have to be the same for us. There is one who mediates for justice and peace and love for all of us. In the family of God, there is a mediator who never fails at his task. When we turn to him, he is able to help us give voice to our anguish; he is able to hear our screams and quiet our hearts; he gives us ease in the midst of pain and above all he opens his arms and receives us with mercy and love and even with forgiveness when we are the cause of the pain that others feel.

That mediator is Jesus, who, when he is allowed to be part of our family systems, can make them function as lovingly and perfectly as the family of God. Jesus mediates the dysfunction in our families and in our lives and replaces it with peace. Jesus restores our broken lives and our distressed families to full and perfect functioning if we ask him. He is ever willing, but we must seek him. Jesus is our mediator, and through him we can have perfect peace and love in our lives and in our families. Through him and with him we are united as the family of God. Don't wait; seek him today.

· 4 ·

FOR THE SAKE OF THE COMMUNITY

NEWNESS AND CHANGE

> *When the day of Pentecost had come, they were all together in one place. And suddenly from heaven there came a sound like the rush of a violent wind, and it filled the entire house where they were sitting. Divided tongues, as of fire, appeared among them, and a tongue rested on each of them. All of them were filled with the Holy Spirit and began to speak in other languages, as the Spirit gave them ability. (Acts 2:1–4)*

Living into my Christian identity, it seemed imperative that I start this chapter with this text that represents the formative event of the creation of a new community. It is considered the recounting of the birthday of the Christian church, and I doubt that this Pentecost text is likely to be considered difficult for preaching. After all, what is there to challenge either the contents or application? It is historical and widely accepted by preachers as the definitive act of initiation of the ministry of the apostles in the name of Jesus Christ.

New Testament scholar Robert Wall, writing in the *New Interpreter's Bible Commentary,* addresses the fact that only Luke provides an account of such an important event, and even then that is succinctly encapsulated in four verses. Luke's intention, he says, is "to move the reader more quickly to the story of the Spirit's powerful effect in the community's mission to Israel, which is more central to Luke's theological program."[1] It is the day that the community, consisting of the apostles and the other disciples, had been waiting for. They had been told by Jesus to wait, and finally the time had come. The waiting was over and the Holy Spirit descended; they were empowered for the work of ministry and evangelism in Jesus' name. Where's the difficulty for the preacher?

In my own preaching as a local church pastor, my approach to this text has been basically as a commemorative fact of Christian history. Pentecost happened, the disciples were energized and empowered, and the Holy Spirit is still here energizing and empowering us for ministry today. It is good theme and a good message (if I do say so myself). But considering both the way in which the understanding of speaking in tongues (which, by the way, was not exactly what happened on Pentecost) has been used to divide the church—those who can, those who cannot, those who believe in tongues, and those who do not—this traditional text may be worth another look. But even more importantly, given the global nature of the church, the multigenerational, multicultural, multisensory, multi-everything nature of society in the United States and across the world, it seems to me that this text presents new or perhaps newer challenges for preachers to look beyond the ecclesial homogeneity (if not of race or culture) of their individual congregations.

Recently, along with several of my students, I spoke with the pastor and attended the worship service of an emerging church. The fledging congregation meets on Saturday night and utilizes the same space as the mother church from which it was spawned. The decorative and liturgical trappings that adorn the altar and the worship space represent a combination of worship traditions and secular decorations and were somewhat fascinating, but what really got my attention was the content of the pre-worship time. For almost an hour different members walked up and down praying loudly and speaking in tongues (as they understood that spiritual gift). The pastor had explained to my class that this time was meant to prepare the space for the worship service, and, in fact, he did not appear until the "warm-up" group was at least forty-five minutes into their praying.

During the course of this warm-up prayer time, one of the persons invited others to come forward and pray and directed them if they did not have a "spiritual language" simply to say, "Jesus." I was startled and fascinated by the directive and wondered at the meaning of "tongues" that prevailed in that congregation. It is a difficult concept that most mainline preachers do not address or even consider. The idea of someone talking in tongues, as it is commonly understood, in one of our mostly middle-class United Methodist Churches is almost unthinkable, and yet this text talks about the community being filled with the Holy Spirit and being given the ability to speak in tongues—languages, if you will, other than their own. What does this mean for the church and how does the preacher address this ability or lack thereof? How does it impact the shaping and the content of community life? Is it an essential criterion of Christian community? One may also ask, is the community at its best if no one has the ability to speak in other tongues than his or her own?

Congregations that consider themselves multicultural face the challenge of meeting the needs of the different cultures in the congregation, usually defined by race or ethnicity and social standing. It has been my contention for some time that—except in rare cases where the church has been reduced to a very small number of persons to the point that it has become a private chapel that caters to a group of elderly who look forward to their and its death—every church is multicultural. Further, every culture has its own language, and through the mix of these cultural languages the congregation develops its own particular language. What complicates this situation even further is that as members come and go, those who have long tenure want to hold on to their familiar language even as young people and newcomers want to add their voices in reframing and reshaping both the language and the culture of the congregation.

The situation is complicated further by the fact that we live in an electronic age and that communications media are changing constantly, sometimes, it seems, faster that the speed of light. Those changes are birthing new words, new languages, new understandings of the world, new requirements of the church and the ever-changing society. The difficulty with this text is in understanding what it means in this day and time to be "filled with the Holy Spirit" so that the preacher and the church can "speak in other languages." If this ability is a gift of the Holy Spirit, then it should be present in the church. It should be present because the Holy Spirit is present, or is she?

There are many places, many churches and congregations, where the Holy Spirit is not completely welcome. There's a sense of unruliness to the Spirit's power that is discomforting in some circles. Wind and fire will awaken many in the church who are happily dozing and are complacently enjoying their comfortable posture of a waiting that has lost its responsibility of watchfulness. On the day of Pentecost the disciples were likewise waiting, but they were also on watch and thus were ready to utilize the promised gift, which enabled "the community, especially the apostles, to testify publicly to Israel" first but then to the whole world.[2] "Luke's symbolism of the Spirit's fiery presence not only signifies the power to speak the word of God effectively but also to think about God in fresh and 'inspired ways.'"[3] And therein lies the difficulty.

LANGUAGE, LEADERSHIP, AND DIVINE DIRECTION

The preacher first but also the entire congregation—the whole church—is meant to be set on fire by the Holy Spirit so that the community can witness to the world in a language that is appropriate to those who need to hear the message of Christ. Contrary to the belief of the well-intentioned sister, there is no need for a spiritual language that no one understands. In fact, the Apostle Paul writing to the early Christian churches made it clear that the gift of speaking in tongues was useless unless there was someone who could interpret the tongues.

> *One who prophesies is greater than one who speaks in tongues, unless someone interprets, so that the church may be built up. Now*

*brothers and sisters, if I come to you speaking in tongues, how will
I benefit you unless I speak to you in some revelation or knowledge
or prophecy or teaching? (1 Cor. 14:5b–6)*

And, yes, everyone understands Jesus, but as a substitute for
speaking in tongues, something seems lacking in the translation.
Preaching this Pentecost text calls for a new or revived understanding
of its meaning in light of the new age in which we live. This is true
for every age, but given the speed at which this electronic age seems
to be changing, the challenge to learn new languages constantly is
one that this popular text calls forth. Because as people and cultures
are changed by the advances of the age their ability to hear the word
of God and to receive the good news of salvation is also changed.
Thus while the contents of the message remains the same, the
preacher's sharpening of language skills is critical. And the good news
in the face of such a mandate is that the Holy Spirit inspires us so
that we have the ability to meet the challenge.

Preaching the same old understanding of the Holy Spirit's mission on the day of Pentecost leaves us floundering, either trying to
learn languages that others have spoken from birth or aping "spiritual" languages without an interpreter in the congregation. The real
challenge for the church, for the pastor and all the people, is to learn
the language that came into being yesterday and be prepared for tomorrow's (almost literal) new language, and that is not easy. This is
not Twitter, tweets, social networks, or blogging. It is the language
of the Spirit that speaks into the hearts of those who need to hear
the message of redeeming love. And the study it requires is not available in a textbook or a classroom or even online; it requires a visit
from the Holy Spirit.

The inbreaking of the Holy Spirit into the community is also
necessary to enable the interpretation of scripture. "Some interpreters
of this passage have heard echoes of Scripture's narrative of the Sinai
theophany and the giving of Torah"[4] to the gathered community.

*When the people saw that Moses delayed to come down from the
mountain, the people gathered around Aaron, and said to him,
"Come, make gods for us, who shall go before us; as for this Moses,*

*the man who brought us up out of the land of Egypt, we do not
know what has become of him." Aaron said to them, "Take off the
gold rings that are on the ears of your wives, your sons, and your
daughters, and bring them to me." So all the people took off the
gold rings from their ears and brought them to Aaron. He took the
gold from them, formed it into a mold, and cast an image of a calf;
and they said, "These are your gods, O Israel, who brought you up
out of the land of Egypt." (Exod. 32:1–4)*

It's a scene of revelry and excess as the people make music and dance
around the golden calf that Aaron has forged of solid gold. The pro-
fessionalism and splendor of Hollywood brought to bear on the
movie *The Ten Commandments* have given many of us, certainly those
of my generation, a picture that speaks of a community gone mad,
lost in the throes of lust-filled excesses. It is the community gone
wild, the people are out of control, and the leadership is lost.

Here also is a text that is not generally preached in churches, although it appears in the lectionary, and that most preachers would
bypass, denying its relevance for the church today. But the notion of
melted bling (to use a vernacular term) being the god of the community is, in my estimation, an appropriate, even necessary subject for
preaching, especially in the face of the prosperity gospel that has become prevalent in many places in the church. But it is not only that
movement that calls this text to our attention; in too many churches
the finances take first place in the minds of the people and the
preacher. Granted, in an economy that challenges the church's financial resources and the people's stewardship, attention to the evidences
of financial health is important. Even so, such attention is only a short
step away from worshiping a golden calf.

What then does this text offer beyond a whole lot of trouble in
the community? If nothing else, it speaks to the power and the responsibility of leaders and the need for good direction as critical to
community health. Moses has been gone for forty days and forty
nights and there is a vacuum in the place that he filled in the life of
the community. Not only that, but without Moses the people have
no access to God. Moses operates as more than the leader of the

community; he is the people's link to God. So their desire for a medium can be understood and even applauded because it speaks of their acceptance and need for a god to have an established place in their life together. Without a god to worship, their religious life falters, as does the source of their power and success. Without a god, they have nothing around which to build community. Their appeal to Aaron, the "associate pastor," and his desire to respond to their need is somewhat commendable, except that Aaron has been with Moses from the start of the journey and should understand the nature of the "I AM."

The challenge of dealing with the trouble of this text is that there is rarely a visible image that the people worship. Leaders like Jim Jones (of "Kool-Aid" fame—the 1978 People's Temple mass suicide in Guyana) and David Koresh (of the 1993 Waco, Texas, seige) lose themselves as leaders of the community and take on the identity of god to the community. Preachers who tout a prosperity gospel are not of the same mind, since in most cases their golden calf is the money and valuables and even the power that they represent or bring that the people are directed to worship. Yet the problem of community worship gone awry is the same. The members of the community offer themselves and the little they have on the altar of the "more and better" that they are convinced their worship will bring.

Now, I am not advocating that preachers use this text to chastise or even address other church leaders, regardless of their focus. There are golden calves much closer to home that need to be destroyed. As stated earlier, the issue of money is one that plagues most congregations, even those that boast large membership or wealthy congregants. Somehow in the church there is never enough, and leader and people find most of their time, both ministry and meeting times, taken up with the issue of money. If this is not worshiping the golden calf, I don't know what is. And the trouble of leadership by those who help in the creation and support the worship of the calf is that they have lost sight of the God who is the true leader of the community.

No longer is the pastor the means of access to God. That is the place Christ holds, so the people do not need an idol, visible or invisible, on whom to lavish their worship. If in their worship of God the people give, not the trinkets that they can well do without, but instead give their all to God, there would be no need to focus on finances, no need to give so much attention and care to money.

> *Bring the full tithe into the storehouse, so that there may be food in my house, and thus put me to the test, says the Lord of hosts; see if I will not open the windows of heaven for you and pour down for you an overflowing blessing. (Mal. 3:10)*

Unlike the Exodus text, this word from Malachi is one that is preached in many churches, but it seems to have little effect. It is not as difficult for pastors to preach because of the issue of tithing, which has come to be understood as a tenth portion of one's substance. (Before or after tax? That is the question, isn't it?) But perhaps if its message is given in combination with the picture of a misapplied allegiance, it may strengthen the message. Certainly the resulting punishment brought to the Hebrew children will not help.

> *Then the Lord sent a plague on the people because they made the calf—the one that Aaron made. (Exod. 32:35)*

One may well wonder if the plague has not already hit, as more and more congregations are dying off, starved for nourishment to feed soul and body. The community is suffering, and many say they have given all that they can give. Focusing the attention of the people on the trouble in the community through a text such as the making of the golden calf is but a step, perhaps a quick-step, in leading them to the worship of the one true God who directs not only our individual lives, but also the life of the community. Because the language of idol-worship suggests pictures of uncivilized peoples, dwelling on the calf, even as an analogy, is the same as speaking in a foreign language. Modern day imagery is critical to bring alive the pictures and grab the congregation's attention.

God was so angry with the fickleness of the people that he threatened to destroy them. In a bold move, the like of which more pastors should emulate, Moses appealed to God on their behalf. Good news! God relented, and Moses was directed by God to come down from the mountain and resume his leadership of the people so that they could find their way back to God. Moses not only resumed his leadership but he had clear direction for the people because he had spent time with God. That seems to be the good news and the message for the community. God directs the community. Be sure that the one who is leading you is taking direction from God. Through Christ each person is privileged to receive divine direction and divine grace to follow God's leading. It is a reminder that the good news of the text emanates from the contents of the text but is resident in all of scripture.

LIVING THE GOOD LIFE

> *"You have heard that it was said, 'An eye for an eye and a tooth for a tooth.' But I say to you, do not resist an evildoer. But if anyone strikes you on the right cheek, turn the other also; and if anyone wants to sue you and take your coat, give your cloak as well; and if anyone forces you to go one mile, go also the second mile. Give to everyone who begs from you, and do not refuse anyone who wants to borrow from you. You have heard that it was said, 'You shall love your neighbor and hate your enemy.' But I say to you, Love your enemies and pray for those who persecute you."* (Matt. 5:38–44)

Mosaic laws were put in place to provide guidelines for living in community. Some modern readings of the law consign them to legalism, but their function was for shaping community, creating a community that met standards appropriate to the people of God. Jesus understood this, but he understood also that his community had strayed a long way from observing both the letter and the intent of the law. Jesus' instructions that we call the Sermon on the Mount represent a teaching moment, and he moves the idea of community norms to a new and higher level. If the laws were already difficult to keep, moving them up even a notch would make them impossible, or so it seems. And in our present-day society we seem to do whatever we can to circumvent the directives Jesus has provided for living in community.

Recently a friend and fellow clergy member sent me a sermon on this text. His detailed exegesis of the meaning of the admonitions or directives offered by Jesus was revealing but not unknown to me. What caught my attention was his analysis of these texts, which led to the conclusion that Jesus' directives were methods appropriate to a stance of "passive resistance or the nonviolent means against injustice which undergirded the Civil Rights Movement."[5] His conclusion is certainly no earth-shaking pronouncement and most likely has been made by others; however, given the focus of this chapter on community, it caught my attention and added fodder to the reasons I had already concluded made this a particularly difficult text for preachers.

We live in a culture of violence. In this moment of history nations in most of the established regions of the world are engaged in some kind of armed conflict somewhere. Turn on the television and try to find a program that does not support the idea of violence as a norm for our world. Even children's cartoons and certainly electronic games tout violence as necessary to live on planet earth. Parents are directed to consider sibling rivalry as normative and are lost when it escalates into full-scale war in the family. How then does a preacher offer such radical ideas as passive resistance? The text deals with trouble, but in the context of the violence of the world it may signify a portent of greater trouble if its directives are followed.

And yet Jesus requires it of our life in community. It is for the sake of the beloved community, the reign of God on earth, that these words of Jesus must be interpreted and preached carefully. Jesus' teaching is about community building, and that requires deep consideration about the type of community we want to build. Of course, as the church considers Jesus' updated laws, it is also concerned with its place in the larger community. The question is, what will become of the church if it continues to allow its directive of passive resistance to be overtaken by society's violent and oppressive way of being?

The trouble for the preacher lies not only in exegeting text and context correctly, but connecting the two in a way that enables the church community to follow Christ's teaching without becoming victim to those outside the beloved community. Turning one's cheek into the aggressor who delivered the first slap puts you on an equal footing, but how does that work when the blow is really a shot from a gun? Becoming naked after giving up coat and cloak does not bring shame on the corporation that forecloses on your home and takes all your possessions. And in the matter of giving to those in need, given the economic reality of many in the community, many people, even Christians, believe that putting others first is both an impossibility and a waste, because there is little or nothing to give to anyone, or so we say, despite our overwhelmingly middle-class lives. So what does one do?

Jesus says: "Be perfect, therefore, as your heavenly father is perfect" (Matt. 5:48). What is the community's response? What is the response of the beloved community? This is trouble with no good news in sight, isn't it?

It is no wonder that "when Jesus was finished saying these things, the crowds were astounded at his teaching" (Matt. 7:28). And it is long after this text, long after Jesus has wrapped up this moment of teaching, that he is confronted by his disciples, who are so completely bewildered that they ask: "'Then who can be saved?' But Jesus looked at them and said, 'For mortals it is impossible, but for God all things are possible'" (Matt. 19:25–26). That's the good news that permeates all of scripture, both the Old and New Testaments. It is a reprise of the divine/human covenant. The matter of living in true community in the world is possible only with divine direction, and God gives that help freely to all who desire it.

SYSTEMS AND ECONOMIES OF GRACE

A response Jesus made to the disciples addressed earlier in this chapter ("Go the extra mile") was brought to bear on economic and social injustice. This topic is worth revisiting as it connects to the issue of violence and its impact on the community. Violence in any form is oppressive. In our communities the violence that rears its ugly head again and again is generally connected with economics. There are myriad schemes perpetrated on individuals and on society—identity theft, price gouging, corporate wrong-doing and downright fraud. At the same time, we live in a litigious society where greed operates at the deepest levels. Enron and Bernie Madoff are familiar names in this category, but economic violence in the community is at its worst when it is done against the least of these. Economic violence affects individuals and the community at large because on a communal scale it targets those on the lowest economic levels who are often rendered voiceless specifically by their lack of economic capital. Just as physical violence in poor communities is more easily tolerated and is addressed with vigor mainly when it spills over into affluent communities, so also economic violence is more insidious and does greater damage at lower economic levels because its victims are forced to keep silent in fear of further reprisals by the power systems.

> *When evening came, the owner of the vineyard said to his manager, "Call the laborers and give them their pay, beginning with the last and then going to the first." When those hired about five o'clock came, each of them received the usual daily wage. Now when the first came, they thought they would receive more; but each of them also received the usual daily wage. And when they received it, they grumbled against the landowner, saying, "These last worked only one hour and you have made them equal to us who have borne the burden of the day and the scorching heat." But he replied to one of them, "Friend, I am doing you no wrong, did you not agree with me for the usual daily wage? Take what belongs to you and go; I choose to give to this last the same as I give to you. Am I not allowed to do what I choose with what belongs to me? Or are you envious because I am generous?" (Matt. 20:8–15)*

Having preached the good news of God's grace in this parable, it was startling for me to read a different analysis that identified it as trouble and thus difficult to preach in many contexts. Reading Obery Hendricks's exposition of this parable helped to reveal the issue of economic violence and oppression that is embedded beneath the surface of God's grace that the parable has always represented.[6]

One of the disturbing subjects in the political rhetoric of our day is that of immigration—illegal immigration to be precise. Dismissing the reality that all persons (except the very small population of Native Americans who survived the massacres and governmental repression) who inhabit these shores are connected in some way to an immigrant, it is a distressing reality that the issue has taken center stage because, I believe, the major group of immigrants involved are people of color.

The exploitation of poor, economically deprived immigrants continues unabated even while politicians debate unworkable policies. Hendricks notes:

> Most biblical commentators believe that with this parable
> Jesus sought to teach that God's grace is equally available to
> all, regardless of when or how one has come before God's
> throne. But when we look a bit closer, we see that this parable
> . . . is also fraught with the horrors of economic violence. . . .
> The householder that is thought to represent God . . . is
> haughty (v.4), insulting (v.6), and dismissive (v.14). Worst of
> all he is exploitative, not only because the denarius a day he
> offers the workers is not a living wage, but because by even
> offering such an inadequate wage he knowingly exploits their
> desperation. After all, given the high unemployment re-
> flected in verse 3, the workers would have no choice but to
> accept his terms, and he knew it. Therefore when read on its
> own terms, it becomes clear that Matthew 20:1–16 is less
> about extolling the benevolence of God's grace than about
> decrying economic violence and exploitation.[7]

Hendricks's treatment of this parable of the Workers in the Vineyard
is particularly poignant in light of the similarity of its situation to
that of so many immigrants in the United States. In many large cities,
such as New York and in wealthy suburban towns such as those on
Long Island, this scenario is played out daily. There are known gathering places to which men arrive early in the morning hoping for a
day's work to feed their families. The violence to the spirit each time
one is not chosen is incalculable. In addition there is often mistreat-
ment of those who are chosen, not to mention the injustice of having
persons work without the minimum of health care or social benefits.
The preacher in today's society is hard pressed to call the congregation to look beyond the ease of knowing that God's grace is theirs
regardless of their time in the church, to making the connection of
Christ's teaching to the present issues in society.

Beyond the grace, or perhaps beneath the grace, that this text affords is the trouble that it reveals. No longer can the good news be

offered without addressing the pain and suffering of those who find their identity in the situation of the vineyard workers. Hendricks contends, and I agree, that by stating the conditions that he did the parable becomes "a profound expression of Jesus' case that the real needs of all who labor should be treated as holy."[8] For the sake of the community as well as for each individual's well-being, Jesus considered each person as holy. In his teaching as well as his healing, Jesus connected with the holy place, the spark of the divine that resides in each individual. It was the reason that he did not shun lepers, fear the demon-possessed, underestimate women and children, or give preferential treatment to those who considered themselves or were considered the privileged of his society. The healing stories reveal a depth of care for individuals that extended to his understanding of the meaning and importance of community to each. Without community, which was denied those with particular illnesses, there was no wholeness for these individuals. And their absence from the community made it less than whole.

JUSTICE, HOLINESS, AND WHOLENESS

The hierarchical structure of Jesus' context was as unholy as that of today's society. Demonic possession, possibly today's schizophrenia or bipolar disorder, kept those so stricken outside of the community. The blind and crippled had no place in the worship of the temple, and lepers, even outside the city gates, were required to announce their presence lest they contaminate the unwary traveler. To all of these their rejection from the community represented a loss of their humanity. The community itself, whether it recognized or accepted it as such, was made incomplete without all who should have had a place in it. The disenfranchised today, the ones whom some would keep outside of the community, range from the mentally ill to HIV/AIDS infected persons, and even to nonheterosexual persons. In other contexts single people, single heads of households, and persons of other ethnic identities or language may be rejected from certain societies. And then there are the poor and economically disadvantaged, who are often treated as less than human and thus unholy. Jesus' healing ministry was to all of these individually, but also for the sake of the community of which they were rightly a part. It was a matter of justice that still calls for attention in the troubles of the world.

> *Now there was a woman who had been suffering from hemorrhages for twelve years. She had endured much under many physicians, and had spent all that she had; and she was no better, but rather grew worse. She had heard about Jesus, and came up behind him in the crowd and touched his cloak, for she said, "If I but touch his clothes, I will be made well." Immediately her hemorrhage stopped; and she felt in her body that she was healed of her disease. Immediately aware that power had gone forth from him, Jesus turned about in the crowd and said, "Who touched my clothes?" (Mark 5:25–30)*

The disciples' bewilderment at Jesus' question is proof positive that they did not understand the nature of his ministry. "Release to the captive" (Luke 4:18b) included persons held captive in situations not of their own making, captive to sickness, disease, apathy, indifference, exclusion and all the ills of body, mind, and soul individually and corporately.

The healing of the woman with the issue of blood (as the KJV names her) is often preached as an issue of faith. Her faith gave her the courage to reach out to Jesus for healing, therefore the message of good news is that by reaching out in faith, we too can experience the healing necessary for our lives. What we miss in the trouble that this woman has faced is her lost-ness. It is the rare preacher who has not done even limited exegesis that provides the information about her culture and recognizes that she had no place in the crowd, being unclean, and that by touching the rabbi, a move not permitted, she made him unclean as well. But it is just as rare that a preacher will delve too deeply into today's untouchables and the systems that keep such persons from reaching the help they need.

At the beginning of his presidency, Barack Obama took on the issue of universal health care for the United States. It is still baffling to me that so many people, politicians and ordinary citizens, protested against it. A student in one of my classes challenged me because I suggested that it was an issue that Christians should support. In response to his accusation that I was politicizing I reminded him that Jesus took on the establishment on behalf of the oppressed and the voiceless and that it was the task of every Christian to do the same. That religious people, self-avowed Christians, would demonstrate against the issue, claiming that health care was not a right for every person, and that states would split hairs claiming inappropriate federal demands on states, and that the leaders of such movements would in the same breath sing praises to God is unfathomable to me.

So many in today's society are like the woman in Jesus' company and simply want their humanity recognized, their name known, and their holiness respected. It's a matter of justice, and good news preaching offers the congregation more that a promise of Christ's healing based on their active faith; it informs them of the present witness of God's grace in their lives as each is recognized for his or her individuality as a child of God and the right to be in the company of all God's people exercising her or his gift of full humanity. That makes all of them holy in the sight of God. Not only that, but it also reminds them of their responsibility to recognize the humanity and the holiness of every other person. That is what Jesus was about when he called the woman forward by asking his question. To Jesus, she wasn't just an accidental encounter, she was a witness to the humanity that names each person as a claimant of a holy identity and a full member of the community of God.

The preacher who chooses to preach good news beyond the norm will bring to light the deep troubles of our world and the deeper love that God gives to each as a person recognized fully by God. It is a witness of the transformative work of God's grace that reaches past the obvious to bring about change that is soul stirring and life renewing.

> *But a man named Ananias, with the consent of his wife Sapphira, sold a piece of property; with his wife's knowledge, he kept back some of the proceeds, and brought only a part and laid it at the apostles' feet. "Ananias," Peter asked, "why has Satan filled your heart to lie to the Holy Spirit and to keep back part of the proceeds*

of the land? While it remained unsold, did it not remain your own? And after it was sold, were not the proceeds at your disposal? How is it that you have contrived this deed in your heart? You did not lie to us but to God!" Now when Ananias heard these words, he fell down and died. And great fear seized all who heard it. (Acts 5:1-5)

It is the stuff of nightmares—the kind of trouble that no thinking preacher willingly unleashes from the pulpit. A preacher who dares to preach this text opens him or herself to the accusation of scare tactics to get members to give more. If you cheat God you will die! That seems to be the logical conclusion, and no amount of exegesis will deny the fact. Ananias died, and it happened as soon as Peter accosted him about holding back funds that he was supposed to give to the church.

That's my story and I'm sticking to it. But can I? Can you? What really happened? Yes, this is major trouble for the church. Can there be some good news to redeem the text? I have never heard it preached, and I have never preached it, and it does not appear in the Revised Common Lectionary. And yet it is a story I learned in Sunday school. Of course Sunday school is not the same as when I went three or four decades ago. But the story remains and it speaks about life in community. What are the responsibilities of communal life?

Now the whole group of those who believed were of one heart and soul, and no one claimed private ownership of any possessions, but everything they owned was held in common. (Acts 4:32)

With that statement we are given a picture of community life. It is the community of believers; and the community operates effectively and successfully because all members believe the same. There is great power and great danger in that statement. It is a feature of the culture of the United States that freedom of speech as a right of every person allows persons who have like minds that promote evil to have the same protection under the law as persons who together promote good. This New Testament community lived in a spirit of love as a community of believers in Christ, loving God and neighbor and demonstrating that love in sharing their resources. It was not a coercive society. It was not even egalitarian; it was Christian and they were guided by a rule of love that considered truth essential to their life together.

The potential breakdown of community that can be caused when one member betrays the covenant is what is demonstrated in this text. It is not for the faint-hearted, preacher or congregant; it is serious stuff that brings to light the essential nature of unity in community. There is an unwritten and generally unspoken covenant that enables the community to function effectively and as the beloved community in Christ. Focusing on the death of this couple is not the heart of the sermon. It was the breaking of the covenant that brought about Ananias' death and eventually his wife Sapphira's death, and it is a reminder to all to beware of the death-dealing systems that can affect community life and bring it to an end. Take, for instance, the clergy person who verbally abuses the associate pastor, the church's administrative assistant, or the choir member, or worse yet betrays the pastoral office by sexually abusing a counselee. And what about the church leader who rides roughshod over everyone's ideas or opinions and makes every meeting a nightmare as it becomes a battleground with that leader on the attack?

A clergy friend shared with me his experience of having to remove a man who verbally abused two women in his church community on several occasions. The situation was so dire that eventually he told the man that he could not be on the church campus at any time but worship and would be accompanied by an usher to his place and accompanied to the boundaries of the church grounds at the end of worship. Of course, the man absented himself from the church but the pastor called the other churches nearby to warn them and called the neighbor pastor who had known about the man but had not warned this pastor. To use my friend's words: "He became "as dead" to us in order to preserve the safety of the community." Although my friend considered this an extreme example, I did not, because of my own pastoral experience and my knowledge of similar situations and behavior among members of the church. In one case the covenant-breaking was so excessive that one of the leaders stabbed another in the middle of a church council meeting. Fortunately the victim did not die, but the perpetrator became as dead to that community.

And of course there are too many situations of persons, both lay and clergy, who have broken the community's covenant by embezzling the funds of the church, by their unwillingness to allow the ministries of the church to flourish simply by their overwhelmingly negative attitudes, and by breaking the spirit of other members. In such cases it is difficult for the community to see or experience the blessing of life in community. God blesses our life in community, when those in the community keep covenant with God and with one another. Christ's presence actively working in individuals and in the corporate life makes of us the beloved community. That's the good news for preaching. The reality of death may be to the community when one person is allowed to break the covenant under which the community lives and works. On the other hand it may necessitate death to the person who would destroy the unity of the congregation's communal life for the sake of the community. That's an important message for the preaching of this text. It's an important message for our living in the world as the beloved community under the lordship of Jesus Christ.

There is joy in the unity of covenantal community living. From the beginning, God made us for each other, and God formed us into community and provided leaders who, with God's direction, would guide the community in the way of life that God intends for God's people. The blessing of community living is in part the companionship that it affords as each does the work of Christ and together the community shows the face of God to the world. Christ in his love unites us with God. We are one through the Spirit of God that blesses us with grace to live in unity—in community with Christ and each other.

THE SERMON

> Then Peter came and said to him, "Lord, if another member of the church sins against me, how often should I forgive? As many as seven times?" Jesus said to him, "Not seven times, but, I tell you, seventy-seven times."

[The Parable of the Unforgiving Servant]

"For this reason the kingdom of heaven may be compared to a king who wished to settle accounts with his slaves. When he began the reckoning, one who owed him ten thousand talents was brought to him; and, as he could not pay, his lord ordered him to be sold, together with his wife and children and all his possessions, and payment to be made. So the slave fell on his knees before him, saying, 'Have patience with me, and I will pay you everything.' And out of pity for him, the lord of that slave released him and forgave him the debt. But that same slave, as he went out, came upon one of his fellow slaves who owed him a hundred denarii; and seizing him by the throat, he said, 'Pay what you owe.' Then his fellow slave fell down and pleaded with him, 'Have patience with me, and I will pay you.' But he refused; then he went and threw him into prison until he should pay the debt. When his fellow slaves saw what had happened, they were greatly distressed, and they went and reported to their lord all that had taken place. Then his lord summoned him and said to him, 'You wicked slave! I forgave you all that debt because you pleaded with me. Should you not have had mercy on your fellow slave, as I had mercy on you?' And in anger his lord handed him over to be tortured until he should pay his entire debt. So my heavenly Father will also do to every one of you, if you do not forgive your brother or sister from your heart." (Matt. 18:21–35)

In 2005 a devastating hurricane hit the city of New Orleans. Subsequent to the hurricane itself the levee system that kept the surrounding waters from overflowing into this city that lies below sea level failed, and New Orleans was flooded. The devastation to the city is recorded as the worst in history from a hurricane, but as I looked at the aftermath of the disaster, I thought that the devastation to the lives of the people was even worse. A few years earlier, in 2003, a tsunami in Indonesia had caused the death of more than 200,000 people from many countries and communities in that area of the world, and although the magnitude of Hurricane Katrina was on a much smaller scale, it seemed to me that the results were the same—communities destroyed and lives lost.

Looking at the television reports on Hurricane Katrina, I was moved with compassion and tears for the people whose lives had been set adrift after the floodwaters receded. I hurt for the people who lost family members in the tragedy and for those who had lost hope of ever again experiencing the vibrant community they once enjoyed. As the murky, diseased waters swirled around homes and in streets, communities were ravaged or disappeared completely; families were torn apart; connections to relatives and friends were lost; and the people were set adrift, rudderless, to find new life and create new communities.

One of the most dreadful happenings at that time was caused when people were thrown together, for their safety, in the New Orleans superdome. The conditions were horrific and there was no one in charge to direct the life of that makeshift community. One of the definitions given by Webster's dictionary for the word community is: "A group of people residing in the same region and under the same government." Certainly the people were residing in the same region, namely the superdome, but what became quickly apparent was that there was no form of government providing the structure for their life in that new place. Not only that, but all the interpersonal relationships that develop over time and are necessary to supporting community life were missing.

Throughout biblical history we see the formation of communities—the Israelites of the Exodus, the people of the exile, and the church after Pentecost. For any community to succeed there must be unity of purpose and will, guidelines, a covenant to which all make their allegiance so that all can thrive. What helps to bring about unity in community is that the members of the community have similar values and outlook, value the relationship between persons and groups, and generally have the welfare of the community at heart. The people thrown together in the superdome were not a community, but they were expected to act like one. They were living together in deplorable conditions; they had simply been thrown into an available space, and, although bound together by the tragedy that had overtaken their lives, they did not have time to develop common under-standing or formulate necessary guidelines to shape the covenant that would enable them to be community for each other as they struggled to survive. It was a disaster of immense proportions.

Matthew's community of Christians is also trying to survive and they have questions about living in community. Scholars believe that Matthew's community was holding meetings separately from the synagogue; hence the word "church" that the gospel writer puts into Peter's mouth. The belief is that this church had its own structure of discipline, its own rules about community and life together in Christ. In fact, the whole of Matthew 18 is about "Life Together," as the *New Interpreter's Bible* names it—life in community. So in order to provide an answer to one of their questions in a way that his com-munity would accept without question, or (said another way) to au-thenticate the disciplinary requirements of his church, Matthew tells a story—or rather, Matthew has Jesus tell a story.

As Matthew's Gospel records it, Peter asks a question and Jesus answers with a parable. "Lord, if another member of the community does me wrong again and again, isn't there a time when I can just walk away from that person forever? Can I Lord? Can I? Do I have to forgive and keep on forgiving that person?" Jesus does not answer Peter directly. His focus is not simply on individual forgiveness, or one person's relationship with another. No. Jesus is concerned with the nature of forgiveness and its impact on community life. After all, that is Matthew's concern, is it not? It should be our concern as well as we live in a litigious society, where it's quicker to take someone to court that to take that person into your heart.

Jesus tells a story that speaks of forgiveness in community. He presents to us a picture of a king. The nature of the king is grace-full, one that forgives a debt of incredible magnitude. Bible scholars con-sider the figure ten thousand talents as incalculable, much too large for our minds to fathom. Perhaps it's simply too large for the king to count. And in the blink of an eye, at the confession and repentance of the unfaithful middle manager, the king says, no problem. This king rules with compassion. This king is the epitome of grace—boundless, amazing love. And the citizens of the kingdom are expected to take their lead from the king and engage their fellow citizens in the kingdom with that same grace. Is that not what life in community is all about?

But wait a minute, where is that great grace when this fellow slips up? Where is that compassionate forgiving king when the forgiven servant fails to forgive? Did not Jesus say seventy times seven, or as the NRSV Bible translates, seventy-seven times? Something is wrong with that amazing grace. Or is it? Now Matthew jumps the gun in the telling of Jesus' story and turns the parable into an allegory by making the king God, and the servant one of the members of the church. But don't get sidetracked too easily; stay with Jesus a bit longer. What is *Jesus'* message?

Remember, Jesus is not talking simply about forgiveness of one person by another. Jesus is talking about the "kingdom of heaven." Those who will be citizens of that kingdom must take their lead from the king. They must be persons of grace also. The kingdom of heaven, the community of God, is inhabited by those who understand that it exists in a circle of grace. That circle begins and ends with God, the author of all grace. Jesus included among his companions sinners, prostitutes, tax collectors (Matthew was one), the rejected, women, the downtrodden. His grace extended like his arms on the cross to whoever will, but his message so palpably present in this parable, is that God's grace not only extends to all but that all are called to be both receivers and givers of grace. It is critical to the life of the community. It is the glue that holds the community of Christ together. Don't count how many times you have to, just forgive.

That's a hard message for most of us to receive. In our individualistic society, we live a mine/yours life. I want what is mine. Mine is not yours and if you take what is mine, you can expect my wrath. But that's not the community of Christ. That's not the community that is the kingdom of heaven; best of all, that's not how the grace of God works. In that community there is no limit to forgiveness; there's no keeping track of how many times. It's not even as one of the bishops of my church said to me some time ago as we discussed the preaching of this parable, that you forgive until you stop counting. It's that you never start counting. You simply forgive.

Wow, that's hard. No, that's very hard to do. Just forgive? In our world? That means anarchy, doesn't it? Not so, says Jesus. Don't even think about counting; and when the whole community does the same, then we will know that the reign of God, the kingdom of heaven, has come on earth. That's the rule by which Christ operates and by which those he calls his own are to operate. And best of all we do not have to rely on our own strength of will or good feeling to do it. God's grace is available, always, enabling us to forgive. When our community is led by Christ, true forgiveness will not be a problem, because when we live in Christ, God's grace is the foundation of our lives and the means by which we can be a forgiving people.

Do you get it? In the kingdom of God grace abounds; and all are united by the grace of God. All of us have been called by Christ into community. So what are the rules? How do we live together? Christ is the head of the community we call the church, and he sets the rules for our life together. As long as we proclaim Christ as head of our lives, we are part of a great community with Jesus Christ as head. All are equal in the community of grace, and all have the same responsibility to emulate the sovereign and to be persons of grace. That is what Jesus tells us in this parable.

It is not easy to do that. It is not easy to show grace to someone who deliberately and cruelly causes you pain, who makes life difficult. It is not easy to exhibit grace when you are the victim of discrimination, when racism, sexism, homophobia, ageism, and all the other isms of life in this world beat down upon you. When it seems like others in the community, even just one person, have so ignored their responsibility to community life and health that you feel mistreated and abused. It is not easy to forgive; it is not easy to refrain from counting how many times you have let things pass.

But that's the rule, and that's where the good news "Father, forgive them" comes in. Matthew makes the parable a sort of tit for tat. The forgiven servant refuses to forgive, so forgiveness previously offered is withdrawn. And as we consider the words of the Lord's Prayer, we too might believe it is indeed simply "forgive us our debts as we forgive our debtors." But that's not what Jesus is about. Our Savior calls to us in the fullness of love, forgives us, and so enriches our lives that by his grace we can forgive. He offers us grace in abundance and, when we accept it, it so fills our hearts and our souls that we can live in love and forgiveness with all those in the community.

As a woman, as a black woman, as a black clergywoman, as a black clergywoman who is a seminary professor, as a black clergywoman seminary professor from a Caribbean culture that teaches you to speak out in a way that is not always understood, it is God's grace that enables me to be in community, to live in community, forgiving and being forgiven for things I have done, things I have left undone, things attributed to me that I have not done, with persons who, in their uniqueness, experience much of the same feelings that I do. And for all of us, Christians, who live in this world, it is the grace of God that enables us to live as members of the community of Christ our Savior. God's grace enables us to be who we are called to be as Christians, forgiving all and always, for the sake of the community. Not only that, but it is God's grace that assures us of our place in the kingdom of God. The realm of God is a place of grace, a place where we live and move and have our being as children of God, saved by grace, where, instead of keeping count of the wrongs done to us, we keep a covenant of love by offering forgiveness again and again and again. It is the way of grace that we are empowered to live as members of Christ's community. It is not in our ability to do it. It is the grace of God alone that enables us to claim our place in that ultimate community with Christ forever. So, Lord, if another member of the church sins against me, how often should I forgive? As often as my grace enables you to forgive; and that is always and forever.

· 5 ·

LIVING A HOLY LIFE

A DIVINE DWELLING

You shall be holy to me; for I the Lord am holy, and I have separated you from other peoples to be mine. (Lev. 20:26)

So you shall remember and do all my commandments, and you shall be holy to your God. (Num. 15:40)

For you are a people holy to the Lord your God; the Lord your God has chosen you out of all the peoples on earth to be his people, his treasured possession. (Deut. 7:6)

Do you not know that you are God's temple and that God's Spirit dwells in you? If anyone destroys God's temple, God will destroy that person. For God's temple is holy and you are that temple. (1 Cor. 3:16–17)

There are many reasons that may make any of these texts and the topic of holy living difficult to preach and difficult for congregations to hear. The idea of the people of God being holy has traveled through time and history and is part of our Judeo-Christian heritage. Again and again the priestly writers reminded the people of Israel of their chosen-ness and the mandate of holiness as the people of a holy God. So Paul's directive, reminder, or warning (however one receives it) to the church at Corinth is a familiar mantra to the Jewish converts. It is most likely not as familiar to the Gentile Corinthians, and in fact greater emphasis is placed on the idea of the Christian being God's temple—the place where God's Spirit dwells—than on the notion of holiness, in part because of their notion of the split between flesh and spirit and also because of their cultural familiarity with the temple as the dwelling place of the gods.

Although Paul does not specify what type of actions will cause desecration, the need to maintain a life of holiness is clear in the warning about God's punitive action if one disregards the mandate to maintain one's person—body and spirit—as a fitting habitation for God. That in itself is problematic for many people who want to think of God as a benevolent father (in the image of Santa Claus) who loves and forgives all people, regardless of their repeated sins. To think of God as the author of punitive action toward people is an unacceptable image for many people, an image that, if at all necessary, should be relegated to the Old Testament. It's a problem for preaching in the twenty-first century.

Further, in a culture where being holy is met with derision and holiness is considered almost synonymous with weakness, the call to holy living is often hard to hear. Generally the expectation of holy living is associated with persons who have made a public declaration of their religiosity, which is erroneously considered synonymous with holiness. Among Christians the criteria for holy living is often subject to the fulfillment of their desires for wealth, recognition, power, and all the "good" things of life. If in the process of gaining these elements of what they consider a successful life they are required to bypass or bend the rules of holy living, it is generally considered a necessity and little attention is given to the breaking of covenant that their actions represent. Individuals and the congregation as a whole may have taken a stance for their own survival that may be a direct contradiction to the requirements of their Christian witness. For example, they may decide not to welcome the new residents of their city because the newcomers are of a different race or culture. Further, the idea of sin as the breaking of God's law is given very little play in the pulpits of many mainline churches, and preaching holy living generally suffers the same fate.

On the other hand there is the violence done to body and spirit by the response that is made to persons who are considered different than some preconceived norm and by the many ills and injustices of society that confront the people of God and make it difficult for them to follow the tenets of holy living. Further, the response to injustice may be seen as too risky for individuals or the community to take the action called for as indicative of a holy life or social holiness.[1] In addition, in the process of defining holy living, there is the danger of being judgmental about some aspects of life that the preacher may judge as inappropriate to Christian mores. There is also the danger that the preacher may assume a moralistic stance that leads to the development of restrictive criteria that all persons must meet in order to be considered holy. Preacher and congregation may face these and other issues that challenge the holy living of both individuals and the community and thus represent an even greater challenge for the preacher of this text.

John Wesley offers a helpful word as a beginning point for preaching these texts and addressing the topic of holy living. In approaching this topic for preaching, a preacher may be guided by Wesley's Three Simple Rules:

1. Do no harm.

2. Do good.

3. Attend to the ordinances of God.[2]

Of course Wesley did not stop there but, in his preaching and leading of the people called Methodists, he named several practices that he considered necessary for a holy life as an individual and for the church as the body of Christ. Most of these directed his hearers to engage spiritual practices that were aimed at following the great commandments defined by Jesus, namely love of God and neighbor.

By addressing specifically the call to Christian living the preacher may provide guidance, as Wesley did, toward regular and fervent prayer, diligent and informed study of scripture, receiving of the sacraments as a regular part of one's Christian life, and demonstrating those characteristics that are defined as fruits of the Spirit and caring for others. And while it is important that the preacher not simply ignore the challenge of falling into sinful ways that besets every person, it is critical that the congregation not be made to follow some contrived list of holy acts that offer a guarantee of reward for a holy life. Preaching holy living means balancing the problem of human sinfulness with the curative of God's grace, and the sermon needs to make that plain as the preacher encourages the congregation to recognize their need to follow the commandments of Christ. Some of Christ's messages to his followers, however, may make it difficult for them to hear the call to a life in Christ.

THE LETTER AND SPIRIT OF THE LAW

Do not think that I have come to abolish the law of the prophets; I have not come to abolish but to fulfill. For truly I tell you, until heaven and earth pass away, not one letter, not one stroke of a letter, will pass from the law until all is accomplished. Therefore, whoever breaks one of the least of these commandments, and teaches others to do the same, will be called least in the kingdom of heaven; but whoever does them and teaches them will be called great in the kingdom of heaven. For I tell you, unless your righteousness exceeds that of the scribes and Pharisees, you will never enter the kingdom of heaven. (Matt. 5:17–20)

A student once said to me that she considered the Bible unfinished and that we should be allowed to add more material to it. She prefaced this statement by saying that she considered the book somewhat out of date. That she was a student in the Master of Divinity program preparing for leadership in the church concerned me somewhat, but I decided to give the problem over to the Holy Spirit, who I believed could straighten her out better and more quickly than I could. Of course I did not get off that easily, as the Holy Spirit promptly threw the matter back into my lap, but with some assistance regarding divine inspiration that enabled the creation of the Bible as we know it.

Exegesis of this text tells us that Matthew's people were having problems with the idea of keeping the letter of the law. The placement of this passage in Matthew's gospel, prior to the six antitheses, is meant to provide a foundation for those statements. Jesus as Messiah is fulfillment of the promise, but that does not make either the law or the prophets null and void. In fact, the coming of the Messiah is to be seen as confirmation of the law and the prophets. And this is all well and good for Matthew's community, but what do these troublesome statements say to the church today?

For many if not most ordinary church folk, "the law" is the Ten Commandments. Even some who take the time to read the Pentateuch quickly move past the hundreds of laws that at times seem like a Bible game of Truth or Consequences. And more and more, the biblically illiterate in the pews have only heard of the Ten Commandments and would find it impossible to name more than a few commandments, or even any in some circles, and certainly not in any correct order. The days of memorizing the Ten Commandments as part of Sunday school studies are long gone. And yet the text appears in the Revised Common Lectionary, so how does the preacher wring good news out of such a stern warning? In an era where people balk at any notion of more government and more laws, the preacher's invitation (for that is what it must be) to be part of the community designed by God must connect with the people's desire to attain membership in the beloved community, the realm of God that is both now and not yet.

The commandments and all the related laws given to the Hebrew people were intended to guide the development of their communal life, surrounded as they were by many heathen cultures. Yahweh provided guidelines that would make of them a special people, people of a new covenant, a holy people who demonstrated their holiness in both their individual and communal lives. That new way of life would be defined not only by their allegiance to the one, true

God, but also by the care that they showed to each other, to the strangers in their midst, and to all people. In this way theirs would be a holy life lived by holy people. The human Jesus lived within the tenets of this culture and his earthly ministry was aimed in part at helping the people of his day to meet both the letter and the spirit of these laws in a way that made holy living synonymous with justice for all people.

In preaching the benefits of living holy lives, Jesus in the Sermon on the Mount goes beyond the legalistic language of Torah and describes the results to be achieved by those who live within the laws of God in language that is common to his hearers. They can hear and understand his meaning clearly. It is a model that the preacher of every age is wise to emulate in offering the good news of the beloved community as a living reality for the people of the present in every age. Jesus lays out the rewards of holy living by naming the blessings or happiness that attends those who live just and holy lives. In the full text as it appears in the Revised Common Lectionary, Jesus describes his followers as essential elements of their culture. "You are the salt of the earth. . . . You are the light of the world." (Matt. 5:13a, 14a). They must be both if they are to be the holy people that Christ's disciples are called to be. They must demonstrate justice and holiness in their communal life while adhering to the myriad laws of the Hebrew Scriptures, or so it seems from these words. Not only that, but while their lives as followers of Christ must be visibly representative of holy living, they must also avoid the self-righteous demeanor adopted by the Scribes and the Pharisees, known keepers of the law.

But what are the laws to which Jesus refers? Certainly it is incomprehensible that Christians in this century should be required to study and even memorize the many hundred laws associated with Torah in order to outdo these law keepers. Our understanding of this text may be helped if we adopt a more proactive stance rather than react with disbelief and dismissal. Torah was given to the people of Israel for the purpose of framing their life as a community and for guiding their communal life in a way that provided care and support for all the members of the community. Matthew is trying to address his community's discomfort regarding the requirement of keeping the whole law even as followers of Christ, and, while his teaching has value for the twenty-first century church, the situation is very different because the questions of law-keeping seldom, if ever, refer to biblical law contained in the Torah.

A TRANSFORMED LIFE

The revelation for Christian living that this text offers for present-day Christians is that everything that challenges the sacredness of life matters. All of human behavior that impacts life in the community for good or ill matters, and Christians are called to model a way of living that represents the eschatological community with Christ as its visible head. The law was given and the prophets were sent to guide the people in the way of holy living according to Torah and to help them to find and stay on the path of peace and justice. Thus far that work has not been completed. Even those who have accepted Christ and made a commitment to the way of Christ have strayed into unholy paths and have allowed and participated in acts of violence in the world. Yet there is good news because Christ HAS come!

Christ has come as fulfillment of the law by his real presence in Christian life. The call to exceed the righteousness of those who are representative of the status quo in the leadership of the people of God invites the followers of Christ into a holy way of living and being that is intrinsic to their lives and not simply representative of expected behaviors. It is a concept of discipleship that calls Christians to walk their talk. It is also a challenge to Christians and the church that both find themselves at odds with the world systems in which they are called to live and to which, too often, they owe their very survival. It is a call to radical obedience of Jesus' teaching that is difficult for many, because it gets at the heart of their being, designed as it is to shape them in new ways. And the fact that the attempt at formation that is at the heart of this text is aimed at holy being does not make the challenge easier. Robin Meyers describes the issues of this difficult teaching this way:

Until we experience Jesus as a "radically disturbing presence," instead of a cosmic comforter, we will not experience him as true disciples. The first question any churchgoer should be asked and expected to answer is: *What are you willing to give up to follow Jesus?*

To recover this understanding of discipleship, however, we must confront an enormous obstacle in Western culture: the idea that to "obey" is to lose personal identity and become intellectually and spiritually oppressed.[3]

Meyers' words speak loudly to adherents of Jesus' teaching today particularly because the notion of discipleship has been reinterpreted to emphasize service to other rather than renewal of self. Jesus' call for adherence to the whole law of God is basically a call to self-denial in the interest of fullness of life for all, and that is neither a popular nor, as some (even Christians) might say, a practical theme for living in today's society.

It bears repeating to say that the good news available for preaching in this text is the presence of Christ. Yes, Christ calls and commands a standard of holy living that may seem impossible to some, even many, but the good news is that Christ has come. And our post-Easter, postresurrection faith assures us that not only has Christ come, not only has Christ risen, but Christ is present to enable and guide his disciples in living according to all the laws that require them to love God and neighbor totally, and to offer and receive forgiveness when failure occurs in any area of life.

Living holy does not mean simply doing no harm. Wesley understood this, as his rules testify. Doing good in all the ways that one can leads one to addressing issues of abuse of power and authority, confronting acts of injustice and violence, and seeking justice for those who cannot speak for themselves. Every sermon provides an opportunity to reveal God's active work of transformation in people and systems and in their relationships with each other and with God. The preacher is called to address the keeping of the laws of Christ with specificity that identifies actions and ways of living that transgress the laws, and at the same time offer a word of grace that assures justification when the transgressor seeks repentance. Through such sermons Christians are alerted both to the benefits of God's grace and the challenge of holy living in the world.

> *I appeal to you therefore, brothers and sisters, by the mercies of God, to present your bodies as a living sacrifice, holy and acceptable to God, which is your spiritual worship. Do not be conformed to this world, but be transformed by the renewing of your minds, so that you may discern what is the will of God—what is good and acceptable and perfect. (Rom. 12:1–2)*

This is one of those texts that many preachers jump into with both feet knowing exactly what it says or should say to the listening congregation. The challenge to resist conforming to the world's seductive enticements and to open oneself to the transformative action of God is preached with zest and delivered with gusto. At the same time, the church in its corporate entity takes on the model of corporate business and uses management techniques to accomplish its work in an efficient and cost-productive way. Unfortunately in doing so the corporate requirement of social holiness is as difficult to achieve and maintain as a personal life of holy living.

The challenge to be holy requires more than the often simplistic call for tithe, talent, and treasure that so often accompanies this text. It is a difficult message to unpack to hearers who are bombarded by a society that encourages and even commands their full participation in order to be considered successful and even accepted. Within the congregation there may be persons who are caught up in a lifestyle that devalues the constancy of committed relationships and have liaisons and sexual encounters without serious thought. The community that is their culture speaks louder and more insistently, and the new age of which Paul speaks is often a muted voice. There may also be persons who are suffering from destructive addictions perhaps to alcohol, drugs, or pornography and have not accepted the need to change or to seek help for their situation. In each case the benefit that Paul names, of being attuned to the will of God, is difficult to absorb in light of its sacrificial cost. There are also those who are living a lie by pretending a level of financial worth that is funded by unmanageable debt that carries the by-product of self-destruction and abusive relationships. For them, holy living is one more challenge that can bring them to their knees, not in prayer, but in total despair. They have nothing left of themselves to give—to God or anyone else.

N. T. Wright posits that the body of which Paul writes "is not that it refers to one part only of the human totality, but that it refers to the complete person seen from one point of view. . . . This whole self is to be 'presented' to God."[4] What this means is that the Christian, having experienced new life in Christ and adopted the mode of holy living, brings the whole self—body, soul and spirit—not only into the act of worship, but into all aspects and activities of life. To that extent it is sacrificial, a concept that is not met with ready acceptance even by followers of the one who made the ultimate sacrifice. So hearing the call to sacrifice in the present culture offers the type of challenge that the congregation is unable to hear, far less to accept.

So what is the good news for preaching? John Wesley believed that we are always going on to perfection.[5] The gift of renewal of one's mind offers the opportunity for right relationship with God in one's life in the present and the promise of eternal life with God. The greater news of right relationship with God is the inner peace that it offers. Culture and society present ideologies and norms that engage hearts and mind with troublesome, disturbing, and often disastrous results. They are, in fact, anything but peaceful, and the tensions of keeping up with the ever-changing and often death-dealing situations of life does violence to mind and spirit and leave us battered and bruised, needing the healing touch of God's transformative love. That inner peace that is the assured reward of those who live according to the will of Christ is an offering of unimaginable riches to all who are sunk in the depleting systems of world power. Presented as a gift offered freely by a justifying, sanctifying God gives hope to lives that are caught in the morass of anxiety and despair.

By offering the peace of Christ, the preacher presents to the hearers a gift of divine grace that is immeasurable in its riches and its ability to bring about the kind of creative energy that enables the recipients to live full and engaging lives as holy people, who together help to bring about the reign of Christ on earth. It is a call to a life of holiness as the people of God in the here and now. As Wright puts it, "[T]he Christian calling to radical holiness of life is likewise a matter of inaugurated eschatology, that is, of beginning to live in the present by the rule of what will be the case in the ultimate future."[6] And the preacher, in offering Christ's gift of peace, does so in the assurance of the same faith through which each Christian claims his or her identity.

LIVING IN HOPE

> *So if you have been raised with Christ, seek the things that are above, where Christ is, seated at the right hand of God. Set your mind on things that are above, not on things that are on earth, for you have died, and your life is hidden with Christ in God. (Col. 3:1–3)*

The difficulty in this text is obvious, or at least I think it is. "Forget about today; live for tomorrow" seems to be the message, and that just does not work for everyone (or anyone?). The grace of God seems apparent—or is it? Through Christ we have been raised above the things of our culture and the lures of the world that seek to entrap our minds, so says the text, and that is good news for any and all persons who have found themselves caught in the web of human sin, whether as oppressor or oppressed. But the reality that confronts the hearers is often a life steeped in the morass of overwhelming trouble or anxiety caused by their inability to find their way out of the maze of depressive and death-dealing systems. Easy sounding phrases of good news are met with skepticism as hearers face the real trials and untenable circumstances of life.

The preacher's awareness of the contextual realities guides the journey through the words and historical realities represented in the text so that the present hearers are led beyond the limits of the context to experience the revelation of Christ's presence in their lives in a way that brings order out of chaos and resurrection and renewal out of lost hopes. The trouble of their lives is thus mitigated by the grace-filled presence of God, and the fearfulness of death that overshadows

their situation is dispelled by the light of Christ that glows with revealing fire. That is the good news of the sermon that restores life
even to those who have lost all hope. As the preacher presents it in
current language and phrasing, hearers are encouraged to invite the
presence of Christ into their life situations in honest and new ways.
It may require painful first steps to allow God to speak truth into
their lives, but it also promises relief and restoration of spirit and is
the precursor to renewed life and realistic holiness of heart and life.
It is divine grace, Christ's unending gift to all; it is the source and
center of new life for the individual and for the community.

> *And you who were once estranged and hostile in mind, doing evil
> deeds, he has now reconciled in his fleshly body through death, so
> as to present you holy and blameless and irreproachable before
> him—provided that you continue securely established and stead-
> fast in the faith, without shifting from the hope promised by the
> gospel that you heard, which has been proclaimed to every creature
> under heaven. (Col. 1:21–23a)*

That's what you call a tall order. Some might even say that it's an impossible requirement, that no one could live up to those standards,
even if one lives with an awareness of Christ's presence. How does
one stay holy and blameless in the sight of God? I have known several
persons, some in their late years, who considered themselves so unworthy that they refused to come to Christ's table. The message of
that communion liturgy that I learned as a child, but that is no longer
popular in my United Methodist circles, was one that they could not
receive even though it presented an open invitation:

> Ye that do truly and earnestly repent of your sins and are in
> love and charity with your neighbor and intend to lead a new
> life, following the commandments of God and walking from
> henceforth in his holy ways: Draw near with faith, and take
> this holy sacrament to your comfort, and make your humble
> confession to almighty God.[7]

They could not accept the truth that the sacrifice of Christ was for
all people. And these were persons who knew and recited often the

well-known and popular text of John 3:16. Somehow they were unable to consider themselves to be a part of the "whoever" that John's gospel names as the recipients of Jesus' sacrificial offering. In such cases the difficulty for the preacher does not lie with nor can it be easily overcome by expounding at length or in detail on the text.

And although the message of John 3:16 speaks of the sacrificial love of God as a perpetual offering of divine grace, one of the problems in preaching this passage from the letter to the Colossians is first enabling the hearers to accept the idea that any of their actions could be the "evil deeds" of the text. Beyond that, for some people there is the challenge of the violence they associate with the death of Jesus, and for still others there is an even greater issue of remaining faithful to Christ. That calls for perfection in life, which most people will not even consider possible and therefore not worth the effort. It bears repeating that in order to preach good news at all times, regardless of the context of the hearers or the troublesome nature of the sermonic text, the preacher must accept personally the covenantal relationship between God and humanity that embraces the whole of scripture. The truism that seeing is believing comes alive as the preacher delves into the stories of God's people that give evidence to the covenantal nature of God's interaction with humanity, which transcends their fascination with sin. Certainly there are texts that speak of judgment and punishment meted out to those who have disobeyed the laws of God. However the necessity of holy living that this text requires is not demanded without the promise of divine help.

The hearer who listens for the embedded grace of God will find it in the assurance that Christ's death has been the medium by which reconciliation with God has already come. The preacher who likewise listens to and beyond this text, finds it and shares it with the listening congregation through the supporting stories that bear witness to the truth of the epistle's claim. It is Christ for us that enables us to live holy lives. It is Christ in us that enables us to be holy people. It is Christ who brings about the transformation of humanity estranged from God to make of us the chosen of God. And the great good news is that transformation takes place in the present. This is the message that Paul writes to the early churches as they are in the process of transformation in the midst of an often hostile culture. The necessity for transformation is to bring about holiness for living in those who have achieved the status of the chosen ones through their acceptance of Christ.

HOLY CHOICE, HOLY LOVE

As God's chosen ones, holy and beloved, clothe yourselves with compassion, kindness, humility, meekness, and patience. Bear with one another and, if anyone has a complaint against another, forgive each other; just as the Lord has forgiven you, so you also must forgive. Above all, clothe yourselves with love, which binds everything together in perfect harmony. (Col. 3:12–14)

In our litigious society of the United States this measure of holiness goes way beyond simple difficulty. It represents trouble to those who have been taught directly and indirectly to look out for number one, to stand up for themselves so that others may not take advantage of their good nature. Earlier in this chapter I named the challenge for Christians who strive for holiness as being seen as humble or meek. Those characteristics are considered a sign of weakness in a culture that believes that only the strong survive. Television, radio, the Internet, and highway billboards are rife with advertisers who hock legal services for real or perceived illnesses or grievances. Court dockets are overwhelmed by complaints and lawsuits brought by and against friends, neighbors, family members, corporations, and even churches. A shrug of disbelief may be the normal or anticipated response to these admonishments or directives from Paul. Wright reminds us that holiness is a complex and difficult topic:

> Paul sees holiness not as an optional extra, not as something to which Christians are called while others are allowed to stay in a state of semi-paganism, but as something which necessarily characterizes all those who are renewed in Christ. At the same time, he is a realist. He does not suppose that Christians are able, in virtue of their baptism, the indwelling of the Spirit, or whatever, to live a hundred-per-cent holy life all the time.[8]

The reality is that living a holy life is difficult. It is countercultural or at least it is counter to the culture of the United States and perhaps Western culture in general and maybe even most of world culture. The Christian hears the words, nods in silent affirmation, or proclaims in doxological excitement in response to the preacher, but goes out unconvinced and unable to wear the mantle of holiness beyond the end of the sermon. The identity of Christ's elect is not a badge worn openly lest it be seen and the wearer publicly shamed for the unimpressive statement it makes.

This is trouble of major proportions for the church. It is trouble that has plagued the church for centuries, perhaps even from its beginning. How could it not when its head, Jesus Christ, had such an inauspicious ending to his life, when he is the poster child for public shaming, being hung on a cross. But just as Jesus' resurrection is a cause for celebration, so too is the newness of life in Christ and the grace it provides for a life of holiness. A life of holiness is seen in outward living, but its reality exists in the inward change that marks those who have received Christ and have allowed the newness that Christ brings to permeate their being and so change their inner core that love and forgiveness and peace and joy become the attributes that they no longer need to seek, but that are visible to all.

Not only do such persons live at peace within themselves, but they strive for peace and justice in the whole world. Kindness, compassion, and humility, along with the presence of Christ in their hearts, become a formidable force for good in the world. They no longer are content to seek a life of righteousness for themselves, but they are compelled to seek right living for all people. Oppressed and oppressors are challenged to new ways of living, and the good news of Christ's redeeming love is extended to the whole world. The challenge of being and living as one who has been chosen and who stands out from the world becomes the witness of Christ's saving love for the world. The mantra of holiness takes tangible form "as God's chosen ones, holy and beloved" reach out in love to a broken world, and no one is beyond the reach of that love. Despite the fact that "love" is an overused word that seems to have little real or sustainable meaning for many, and real forgiveness seems an impossibility, that message from the preacher can reach the depths of human shame and depravity and give witness to Christ's presence in the world, offering goodness and mercy and forgiveness and love to all. It is the holy way of living in Christ, with Christ, and through Christ.

FOR JUSTICE AND RIGHTEOUSNESS

One day, as we were going to the place of prayer, we met a slave girl who had a spirit of divination and brought her owners a great deal of money by fortune-telling. While she followed Paul and us, she would cry out, "These men are slaves of the Most High God, who proclaim to you a way of salvation." She kept doing this for many days. But Paul, very much annoyed, turned and said to the spirit, "I order you in the name of Jesus Christ to come out of her." And it came out that very hour. But when her owners saw that their hope of making money was gone, they seized Paul and Silas and dragged them into the marketplace before the authorities. (Acts 16:16–19)

How does one measure a life of holiness; what are the criteria to be applied to one's actions? How do you judge the actions of Paul and Silas and of the slave girl? Or is it fair to judge others by a standard of which they are unaware or to which they have not committed? At first glance it seems that this text says less about holy living than it does about being victimized. Certainly this text seems long on victims and short on justice, a function of holy living. Who are the real victims here and what sort of justice does one preach from this text? And where is God anyway? There is sufficient trouble to go around, but where's the redemptive grace that makes holy living a reality or even a possibility?

Certainly, the young woman is a victim of injustice. She is a slave and subject to the bidding of her masters. Her role in life is to perform for their financial benefit. As a slave she does not own her own person, so any violence done to her is allowable because of her enslavement. That her identification of Paul and Silas as followers of the Christ was not sanctioned by her owners is clear and seems to emanate from an internal source that may well be the intrinsic realization of her worth as a human child of God. One might well conclude that to use her gifts without coercion or compulsion for the benefit of her owners may have been a freeing experience for this girl who is bound in many ways. But in doing so she experiences further victimization and injustice. Paul is annoyed and he responds in anger to the beleaguered slave girl, denying the holiness of heart he is called to demonstrate as a follower of Christ. Scholars compare the girl's behavior with that of demoniac who followed Jesus as he entered the synagogue of Capernaum. Commentator Robert Wall contends that "the slave girl unwittingly has thrown down a gauntlet of sorts to Paul."[9] Whether that is the case or not, it is unintentional and yet she is judged and pays the price of the loss of her skill. That means more victimization, and then the text ignores her beyond that point. She is so much flotsam in the tide of events that involve her owners and the apostles, such that the victimization and the injustice of this unnamed woman continue even beyond the text itself.

There is no further mention of her beyond the fact that without her special gift she is no longer a viable source of revenue for her owners. One wonders what becomes of her and whether the judgment that left her without a source of income for herself or for anyone else is just. The story moves on as it must, given the focus of the biblical record, but it offers a good stopping place for the preacher who is concerned about the many persons, usually women and ethnic minorities, who fall victim to systems that sweep them up in the fast moving current of power-laden affairs and then leave them stranded, lost, forsaken, and alone, with no way of fending for themselves. Since the girl is absent from the rest of the story, what can a preacher do to give life to her situation as a way of connecting with those in society, even those among his hearers who are likewise victimized and tossed aside like so much debris?

I learned a term in one of my preaching classes from an African American student who assured me that it was appropriate for preachers to expand on a biblical story well beyond the limits of the text. He called it using his "sanctified imagination." I imagine that in trying to reframe or expand this girl's story one could use sanctified imagination to give it an acceptable, if not a happy ending. But a definitive statement of good news by the preacher, if it does not emanate from scripture, if its content lacks substance, or if the preacher has subverted the text in any way, lacks credence in its claim regardless of how well it is delivered. Honest admission of the insufficiency of one text is offset by the inclusion of a similar story where the good news is apparent and real.

In this case, following the events surrounding Paul and Silas does not do it. That is a different story with a different theme. Although they are imprisoned, that is different than the enslavement suffered by this young woman. Instead the preacher may connect with Jesus' purpose of releasing the captive, who then receives new life, or even with one of the healing stories of Jesus where the one who is healed is assured of new life. The good news of freedom and justice is located in the divine purpose, and its biblical witness must be both authentic and relevant to text and context. The trouble that surrounds the people of God finds relief only in the present, active grace of God, and this work of grace may be performed by anyone in the name of God. Certainly Paul and Silas were in Philippi to do the work of Christ and, despite the fact that it was anger that caused him to bring about the change in the woman's life, her freedom from bondage could rightly be attributed to the work of the Holy Spirit. In fact, Wall contends that in response to the challenge that the woman unknowingly issued, Paul's "spiritual authority" as a prophet-like-Jesus is thereby confirmed by this exorcism: The Holy Spirit in Paul is greater than the unholy spirit who speaks through the girl.[10] The injustice apparent in this text serves as a catalyst for preaching justice as requisite for a holy life as a follower of Christ.

TO LIVE AND MOVE AND BE IN CHRIST

The issue of freedom of slaves is certainly one of justice, and, although Paul does not do this intentionally, he does face the problem directly in his letter to Philemon.

> So if you consider me your partner, welcome him as you would welcome me. If he has wronged you in any way, or owes you any-thing, charge that to my account. I, Paul, am writing this with

my own hand: I will repay it. I say nothing about your owing me even your own self. (Phile. 17–19)

The subject of slavery in the culture and society of the United States is one that still causes pain in the hearts of some individuals and groups. In fact, some would say the fight for complete freedom has not yet been won and this text is not preached by many, although it appears in the Revised Common Lectionary (Year C, the sixteenth Sunday after Pentecost). The issues of justice and judgment seem apparent. Onesimus is a slave and imprisoned with Paul. One might suppose that he is there under sentence for having broken some law and has been judged guilty. But this is no more true than it would have been for slaves in an earlier time in the United States and for those enslaved in less obvious ways by today's systems and also for the many persons, especially young black men, who find themselves imprisoned without evidence of crime or guilt. Upon release from prison, Onesimus is required to return to his master. He is property of the master and therefore of some value. But Paul is requesting a change of status for Onesimus. In effect he is asking that Philemon give up the value of his property on Paul's word as an apostle and teacher in the faith.

What's in this for Philemon? If he agrees to Paul's request, he loses valuable "property," while Onesimus can celebrate the good news of his freedom. So how is justice served to the parties involved? Does justice require a win-lose ending? Paul promises repayment, but his situation as a prisoner in need of care for his own needs makes that unlikely. How can this text be preached, especially at a time when there are so many incarcerated in jails and prisons, and especially in the very areas of society where the after-effects of slavery are still being felt? Can the church demand freedom for prisoners in the name of Christ? What authority do the followers of Christ have to bring about freedom and justice for the oppressed? In the name of Christ it can and it must. That is the good news that this text reveals, and it speaks of both judgment and justice in the name of Christ. Since the good news of the sermon speaks of God's transformative grace in the life of the people, the preacher who goes into the physical prisons may offer intercession on behalf of the incarcerated so that their souls need not be imprisoned any longer. But it is not only in such places that imprisonment occurs. Many are imprisoned by the trials of their lives and the sorrows of their souls. The preacher offers the good news of Christ's intercession on their behalf that guarantees their freedom to live full and fruitful lives. While those who have been imprisoned in city, state, and federal facilities may have to complete the full terms of their imprisonment in the cause of justice, their hearts and the hearts of those they have wronged can be freed by the good news of Christ's redeeming grace.

There are other texts, however, that seem to offer anything but grace to the oppressed. In fact, they seem to support oppressive systems such as slavery and to invite the marginalization of women and those who might be considered other by the power structures that exist in society.

> *Wives, be subject to your husbands, as is fitting in the Lord. . . . Children, obey your parents in everything, for this is your acceptable duty in the Lord. . . . Slaves, obey your earthly masters in everything, not only while being watched and in order to please them, but wholeheartedly, fearing the Lord. Whatever your task, put yourselves into it, as done for the Lord and not for your masters, since you know that from the Lord you will receive the inheritance as your reward; you serve the Lord Christ. (Col. 3:18, 20, 22–24)*

There are many issues that complicate the challenge of preaching good news from this very troublesome text. The hegemonic use to which these biblical texts, attributed to Paul, have been put begins by ignoring the incompleteness of the message. Biblical scholar Cheryl Anderson writes that this and other similar texts "were probably not written by Paul. Instead, they reflect the concerns of later generations, one of which was the need to emphasize the paterfamilias, the (heterosexual) male-headed family unit, as the appropriate ordering of the household."[11] Such understanding does not mitigate the difficulty for wives who are victimized emotionally, spiritually, and physically by their husbands. The text also challenges women who are single and who desire to fill the wifely role without success.

The text may serve as a reminder of a perceived inadequacy or lack because of their unmarried state. This text may be problematic as well for households that are led by same-sex partners, which do not resemble this model.

Also of great significance and challenge to today's preacher is its historic use in society over the centuries of Christianity and the way in which it has worked to shape modern culture. Postmodernity and its challenge of the notion of absolute truth have done little or nothing to mitigate its influence on the hierarchical construct of society in the United States and around the world. The preacher is faced with an uphill, if not insurmountable battle to reclaim the motif of justice that underlies this text. Preachers may begin the task of preaching good news by helping the congregation to hear the text in its completeness—by bringing to the foreground the missing and complementary verses that make of these household codes of the first century societies a reciprocal experience of care for all in the household.

> *Husbands, love your wives and never treat them harshly. . . .*
> *Fathers, do not provoke your children, or they may lose heart. . . .*
> *For the wrongdoer will be paid back for whatever wrong has been*
> *done, and there is no partiality. Masters, treat your slaves justly*
> *and fairly, for you know that you also have a Master in heaven.*
> *(Col. 3:19, 21, 25; 4:1)*

This is the flip side of the text that may serve as a corrective to the issues raised in preaching; however, it does not address the reality of present-day culture where the roles between men and women in society are being reframed to meet the new structures. Preaching both texts as one does not resolve the problem, but it does help the preacher to address the textual difficulty by faithful, critical interpretation of the biblical message. It also requires that the preacher give serious consideration to the context of the congregation and the society so that the text will speak with relevant voice and thus help to shape the hearts of the hearers for living holy lives.

The call for holy living is as present in scripture as is the evidence of God's covenantal love that enables Christians to respond to that call. But while it is true that the good news of divine grace is as present in the stories of both exile and restoration, slavery and deliverance, capture and release, oppression and freedom, it is difficult to hear of God's retributive justice in the midst of death-dealing situations. It is also well nigh impossible to believe in the eternal love of God when one's experience is that of human depravity at work in the world. Despite this, the Christian witness of holiness of heart and life testifies to the God of love and justice who overcame sin and death so that humanity could live freely in God's love and spread that love throughout the world. It is life in Christ, empowered by the grace of God, that brings to fruition holy living by the whole people of God. That is the message of all preachers, who themselves are called to live holy lives.

THE SERMON

Every generous act of giving, with every perfect gift, is from above, coming down from the Father of lights, with whom there is no variation or shadow due to change. In fulfillment of his own purpose he gave us birth by the word of truth, so that we would become a kind of first fruits of his creatures.

You must understand this, my beloved: let everyone be quick to listen, slow to speak, slow to anger; for your anger does not produce God's righteousness. Therefore rid yourselves of all sordidness and rank growth of wickedness, and welcome with meekness the implanted word that has the power to save your souls.

But be doers of the word, and not merely hearers who deceive themselves. For if any are hearers of the word and not doers, they are like those who look at themselves in a mirror; for they look at themselves and, on going away, immediately forget what they were like. But those who look into the perfect law, the law of liberty, and persevere, being not hearers who forget but doers who act—they will be blessed in their doing.

If any think they are religious, and do not bridle their tongues but deceive their hearts, their religion is worthless. Religion that is pure and undefiled before God, the Father, is this: to care for or-

phans and widows in their distress, and to keep oneself unstained by the world. (James 1:17–27)

As a child growing up, I got myself and my two older sisters in trouble with my mother often because I just could not tell lies well. The three of us would do something wrong, something that my mother had told us not to do or that we knew would get us in trouble, and my oldest sister would swear us to secrecy. We would all agree that, no matter what, we would not tell; but as soon as my mother said—"Gennifer! What . . . ?"—Before she could finish asking the question completely, I would be confessing, telling everything. I don't know why I am still alive and sound in body. My sisters should have simply taken me out of their lives like Joseph's brothers did to him for the tattletale that I was.

Telling the truth has always been important to me—and continues to be so today. Now, telling the truth can get you in a lot of trouble and not only when it comes to admitting wrongdoing. It seems that all of my adult life people have had a problem with the way I speak and act when it comes to truth-telling. I tell my students that they can always expect me to tell them the truth about how they performed as preachers, but that I would try my best to do it in a way that enabled them to receive it. But difficult to speak or hear, or not, for me the absolute truth was what I felt I owed them. Telling the whole truth is part of my moral code, one I have tried to keep all my life, sometimes unfortunately with insufficient care about the impact that the truth would have on those who received it. In this respect you might call me a moralist, someone who lives by a particular moral standard of behavior. And some of you might even be saying, So what, that's what is expected of you, isn't it? Indeed, yes. That is what is required of me and of all of you—all of us who call ourselves Christians. And if we look at the epistle lesson from James 1, we might be tempted to believe that being moral persons is the only thing that is expected of us if our desire is to live holy lives.

Well, you've figured out by now, I'm sure, that I'm going to say just the opposite. And you're right. As Christians we are not called to be simply moralists. In fact, Jesus spent a lot of time and gave a lot of attention in his teaching to dispelling that notion. Again and again we hear Jesus saying, "You have heard that it was said" such and such, "but I say" something else, maybe even just the opposite. Jesus was no moralist. His task on earth was not to call people simply to follow a set of moral laws. In fact, his conversation with the Pharisees recorded in Mark 7 is about just that—following the law and doing just the opposite. No. Jesus came to set us free from having to memorize each of the myriad laws that confronted the people of Israel. It was not that we were to discard the laws; instead he called us to live beyond the law and the prescribed morality of his day.

Jesus called us to live in love as Christians—to go beyond what had been set out as the norm, not simply to disregard the law, but in love to do more than what the law required. Jesus' conversation with the Pharisees struck a pretty sensitive nerve with persons whose every goal was strict observance of the hundreds of laws that was Torah. He called them and us to live holy lives, and one aspect that I want us to consider is to live truthfully, not simply to know and speak the law, even the law of Christ, but to live it in our words and actions. His was a call to live a life that showed love of God by walking in the ways of God; because if people lived in the love of God, then that love would show in their actions with one another. In other words, if they truly loved God, they would naturally love their neighbors and there would be care and compassion within and outside the community reflecting God's covenantal care for all people. When we truly love God, God's holiness is reflected in us and we live in the fullness of that love.

You see, where real love exists, regardless of the type of love or parties involved in the love relationship, there is total truth. True love means truth-telling. Jesus called the Pharisees to live in the truth that they professed in their outward observance of Torah; and Jesus calls us to live the truth of God's saving love that gives us new life and offers us eternal life. It's not an easy way to live, believe me; yet it is the call on our lives, and it offers, no Christ offers, eternal rewards. This is what James is talking about in this passage of scripture. It is what Bible scholars consider to be a moral imperative, which reveals one's Christian identity. That is the focus of James' writing throughout this book of our faith. It is the message that James delivers to every Christian, past, present and future, through this writing and it offers instructions about the way that we should live our lives as persons who are living in truth as disciples of Jesus Christ.

James, believed to be the brother of Jesus, exhorts his hearers to adopt the type of behavior that marks them, names them, and presents them to the world at large as examples of what it means to be Christian. He begins by calling the community to see the trials of their lives as tests of faith that give them strength to endure whatever comes their way in life. Now if you believe what James says, it is important to know that it is not necessarily God who sends all those challenges and tests your way. In fact in verse 16, just before the beginning of today's passage he cautions us. "Don't be deceived." And then he offers us an important truth that is critical to the shaping of our lives as Christians. James 1:17–18 (NIV) says to us: "Every good and perfect gift is from above, coming down from the Father of the heavenly lights, who does not change like shifting shadows. He chose to give us birth through the word of truth, that we might be a kind of first fruits of all he created." In other words, God is good all the time and God created us to be persons who show God's love. Or said another way, right out of scripture: "God so loved the world [all of us] that God gave Jesus Christ, the only begotten Son of God, that whoever believes in him should not perish, but have everlasting life." That is the word of truth that James shares with us. That is the truth that gives us life, new life—life everlasting. That is Jesus Christ, the only truth that we need, the only one who can and does give us all that we need so that we can live according to the Word of God.

Scholars consider that this book of James follows the Wisdom tradition of the Torah, which means that it offers practical wisdom that is meant to guide the community in right behavior. And since this book is inherently Christocentric, that means that its tenets are based on the person of Jesus Christ, that it is founded on the belief in Jesus Christ as Savior of the world, and that the directives it offers come directly from the teachings of Christ. Well, if that is the case, and I believe it is, let's look at what Christ, through this book of James, calls us to live and be; the attitude he calls us to have, as we live holy lives together in community, demonstrating social holiness, under the Lordship of Jesus Christ.

We are because Christ is; our birth as Christians, our new birth that reclaims us from the death of original sin, originates from the life, death, and resurrection of Jesus Christ. And in order to be like Christ, to live in righteousness, we must be "quick to listen, slow to speak, slow to anger." Wow, that's so difficult sometimes. We live in a fast-paced world where people are talking all the time; before you can hear what they are saying, they have moved on and you are left behind wondering what just happened. It's hard to keep up; there's little time for silence—not even in our worship. In fact we are so uncomfortable with silence that in many churches a "moment of silence" means that the organist starts playing background music, or as soon as the time of silence is proclaimed, before you can take a deep breath, the liturgist continues speaking. And so our minds never get a chance to rest and absorb what others are really saying to us or what God is trying to say to us. Sometimes we are so caught up in speaking and trying to get our points across that, in the immediacy of the spoken words, not hearing or understanding their full meaning, we react in inappropriate or unnecessary ways, and too often with anger or hurt feelings that later lead to anger.

Perhaps you know what I'm talking about. You say something out of kindness to help someone and he or she gets so angry that you are lost, wondering what did I say? Or someone says something to you and, because you are not really listening, you hear only a part of what they have really said and you come back fighting when it is not at all necessary. In fact, you hear the words and allow them to be colored by what the world has taught you to hear, what sin in the world has conditioned you to read into the statement of others; and you miss the opportunity to hear Christ speaking to you out of the words of others. You see, if we hope to live in holiness, it means that whatever we hear must be allowed to experience the scrutiny of the implanted word of truth in our hearts; we must allow the love of God within us to be the interpreter of what is being said so that we can hear God speaking through the human words.

On the other hand, before we speak, we must allow that same spirit of God to vet the words we are about to say to someone. James instructs us to be slow in our speaking so that we can allow God enough time to change both the content and the tenor of our words so that, in our speaking, the truth we offer becomes palatable to those who must receive it. Now as I wrote this sermon my heart burned within me because I could hear God speaking to me about my own quickness to speak without thinking through what I need to say, and even worse my quickness to become upset and even angry because of words that are spoken to me. As the folks would say in the little Baptist church I visited years ago, "Speaker is speaking to self."

You see, James names the issue; he gets to the heart of the matter when he says, "Be doers of the word, and not merely hearers who deceive themselves." Too often in our lives, in our homes and our jobs, and worst of all in our churches, some of us, Christians, give the appearance by the words we parrot that we are all that we should be as Christians. And when we think no one is looking, or no one that we want to impress with our goodness can hear us, we act in abominable ways. We pull each other down in conversations that are really just gossip; we rip each other apart to get and hold onto what we believe are positions of power; we spit in each other's faces through the nasty actions that we do against each other; and some of us are even bold enough to curse folk openly. In the church some members act out in unholy ways by holding back our giving to God, withdrawing from the work we are called to do, deciding that we can no longer go to church to worship God because of who we will meet there (not God, of course), and justifying the actions we take by believing ourselves to be more righteous than our brothers and sisters, sometimes even than God.

This letter of James calls us to change our attitudes toward one another; to show mercy and compassion wherever there is the need, and to live in solidarity with each other as we all try to live holy lives in God's sight. It calls us to live as members of the beloved community—the called of God, those gathered in the name of Christ—in a way that shows that we are really one in the spirit of Christ. When we hear the word of God but do not live it, our actions are not representative of our Christian identity. Yes, all people sin and fall short of God's glory; and yes, we, like all Christians, are sinners, saved by God's grace. By our own strength, we are anything but righteous, we are by no means holy, no, not one of us, but because of the amazing grace of God, because of the righteousness of our Savior Jesus Christ, because of the sustaining presence of the Holy Spirit, and only because of the love of God, we are able to live lives of truth and love—to live in holiness and righteousness all our days and thereby lay claim on life, even life everlasting.

It is that assurance, that free grace of God—not our religiosity, not our morality, not the praise that comes from lips—that enables us to live a life of truth and love and justice for all people in word and deed. Only because of Christ, the word of truth implanted in our hearts, can we live holy lives. It is our Christian witness that calls us to say and do the things of God. When our hearts have been purified by Christ and renewed by the indwelling spirit of love that he offers, then and only then can we hope to live lives of holiness. Holy living is living in Christ; it is living in love; it is living by and through the grace of God.

No, it is not easy. No, it does not happen simply because we say so. It happens only because and as long as we allow Jesus Christ to have full possession of our hearts. Jesus alone gives us the grace we need desperately to live in the truth of his Word and so to live in holiness and righteousness all our days. But the most wonderful piece of news that we have as Christians is that that grace is available and free to all who desire it. God's grace is present for us even when we do not recognize it. But when we seek it, it is never far from us. God's grace is ours, available and present to each and every one of us individually and as the gathered community. And by that grace we can speak and hear in a way that makes real Christ's presence in the world. We can live in community in a way that is uplifting and enlivening to others. We can hear what others say, even when the words are not particularly pleasing, and allow God to speak through the words so that anger and hurt do not take hold of us.

I wish holy living was only about what we say and that it was simply not telling lies, or even being able not to be a tattletale. That's for childhood. But James' words tell us it is a lot more than that, and Christ's words instruct us that it is not simply what comes out of our mouths; it is what is in our hearts. My sisters and brothers, as Christians, our call is to be more like Jesus—to love God with heart and mind and soul and strength, to love neighbor as self, to do all things after the example of Christ. That means to speak the truth in love, to live holy lives as Christ lived, and through Christ and in Christ to know the joy of life with Christ now and forevermore.

May it be so through Jesus Christ.

· 6 ·

SAVING GRACE

THE CALL TO PREACH

The call to preach is a divine invitation that rings with compelling urgency in the minds and hearts of those who receive it. The clamor of the holy summons resounds in the ears and echoes in the souls of the prophets of God. It lays undeniable claim to the proclamatory voice of any and all who hear and answer the call. The substance of preaching lies in the interweaving of divine initiative and human engagement. The voice of God rings out from the pages of scripture with resounding force, reaching beyond past memories and future hope to offer transformation and new life as a present reality. It is divine grace that reaches into the troublous depths of individual difficulty and corporate wrongdoing, offering light and life, justice and peace, hope and love and unending joy.

The call of God to the preacher impels him or her to reach into the often unfathomable depths of the biblical story to see the heart of the divine, which is love for the whole people of God. It is an urgent and inescapable call to any and all who would be faithful in offering good news to the people of God. It cannot and should not be dismissed, because the saving grace of God, the ultimate message of the preacher, is the only remedy for human sin. Whether or not the preacher chooses to name the sin for what it is, it continues to infect the hearts of God's people. The pages of scripture offer witness to the trouble that has and continues to influence and plague humanity, and scripture simultaneously testifies to the grace of God that overcomes the trouble encountered in human living.

The call to preach is thus an appeal to the preacher to reach back with integrity into all the pages of biblical witness regardless of the difficulty encountered in addressing their contents. None can be avoided or bypassed because of the treasure trove of divine love they contain. The preacher's responsibility of retrieving the evidence of God's love and offering it to the waiting congregation has remained unchanged over time, even as the call to preachers to speak in the name of God also remains the same as originated with the earliest prophets. The message of scripture is above all good news for the people of God. It resounds with saving love that is divinely initiated and unstintingly offered even in the face of dismissal and rejection by suffering humanity. The task of the preacher in answering the call to preach is twofold. First the preacher boldly and courageously approaches the biblical text with expectation of finding the eternal message that may be hidden in layers of time-honored yet undecipherable prose. Second, the preacher searches beneath the rubble of broken lives and oppressive systems to reach the light of God's love that shines with redeeming brilliance, bringing to blazing life the divine spark that is the soul of humanity.

It is a search for the evidence of God's enlivening, engaging, transforming presence in the midst of human endeavors, and it is essential to the preaching encounter so that the people of God can experience the revelation of divine love throughout time, and that gives them the assurance of that same grace in the present. The call to preach is thus a call to encounter again on every occasion the word of God embedded in the words of scripture; to retrieve that word; and to offer it to the waiting congregation. In the encounter with scripture the preacher may be confronted with challenges of content, construction, and meaning that make the retrieval of the word difficult. The preacher may also be faced with the challenge of delivering the message to persons who have difficulty receiving it. Yet the mandate for preaching good news is the substance of the preacher's call that cannot be bypassed or dismissed regardless of any difficulty in delivering the good news. The source of the good news is God, and the evidence of God's covenantal faithfulness that substantiates the witness of divine love to faulty humanity is found in all of scripture, even the difficult texts.

DIFFICULT TEXTS AND GOOD NEWS

The good news of divine grace shines out of the pages and words of scripture. As those ever-living words are brought into view and connected with the lives of God's people, trouble becomes opportunity for experiencing the reality of God's love, and the assurance of grace becomes a lived reality in the life and community of the people of God. God's grace is as available in the stories of slavery and exile, oppression and injustice as in tales of rescue and deliverance, healing and restoration of individuals and families and communities. It is as present in the historic tales of those who have battled the demonic forces that would separate us from God and from each other as it is in the revelations of filial love and radical hospitality to strangers and outcasts. Good news emanates from the divine engagement between God and the people, between the intersections of human sin and divine grace. Just as it is made visible in the words of scripture, so it must be made real in the sermon so that it can offer a witness that engages the people and brings forth their own testimony.

Connecting the trouble of the biblical text in relevant and imaginative ways with the present context is the task of every preacher for every sermon. Making the text come alive to the changed circumstances and the even more quickly changing faces of life calls for new searching, new methods, new engagements, new analyses of both text and context in order to extricate the embedded good news. The requirement for preaching good news in every sermon is predicated in the belief that the hearers need new and fresh supplies of grace in order to meet the continuing and new challenges of life. Recognizing that some passages of scripture do not easily relate or transport good news, the preacher who subscribes to the efficacy of using all of scripture for engaging and directing humanity in Christian living is faced with the challenge of making even difficult texts available to the congregation.

When it comes to finding and preaching good news from a difficult text, having a theology of good news is essential. Unless the preacher approaches the text with that mindset, it may be impossible to see beyond the words or even the situation of the text to the mitigating presence of God. The writer of Hebrews assures us that "[God] Jesus Christ is the same yesterday, today, and forever," (Heb. 13:8) and that sameness has to do with divine grace that is ever present to engage human life and overcome human sin. Not only that, but the essence of grace that permeates the Godhead offers assurance, despite evidence that seems contradictory, that God's love prevails in all circumstances both in scripture and in the world.

A theology of good news is an essential tool in the preacher's interpretative arsenal. Its impact in the shaping the preacher's life gives important direction in the search for good news. To reiterate, it primes the pump, so to speak, so that the preacher not only expects, but is prepared for the revelation of grace that is embedded in the overarching story of redemptive grace that is the Bible. It opens the door to understanding the context of preaching by enabling the preacher to approach the congregational context and hear the needs of the people through the grace of God present in the text. The meeting of the text and the context of the hearers creates a location for offering the good news of the transformative love of God.

Not only is a theology of good news foundational when the goal is an offering of transformative good news to the hearers, but so is knowledge of the preaching context. Let me reiterate that the good news is God's active transforming presence in human endeavor. It is not a sinecure that ensures happy, smiling faces in the midst of trouble. Instead it is the assurance of God's active, empowering, enlivening, and transforming love that provides needed support and guidance in the midst of life. Whether or not the preacher has pastoral responsibility for the hearers of the sermon, some sense of the situation locally and globally that impacts the lives of the people is necessary. This knowledge helps the preacher to shape the sermon in a way that allows the hearers to feel that the preacher understands who they are. Hearers want to experience a connection with the preacher and to engage the substance of the message in a personal way that helps to support their Christian discipleship.

Preaching good news requires that the preacher not only believes but also lives in the assurance of divine grace. The ongoing relationship between God and the preacher is the source of that assurance, and when it is a lived reality in the life of the preacher, then offering the gospel in every sermon becomes foundational to the homiletical theology and practice that undergirds the creation of the sermonic message. The good news of divine grace that operates in the life of the preacher finds resonance in the biblical story, even the troublesome stories, and is expressed through the words of the sermon and specifically in the message of good news that is the heart of the sermonic message.

The challenge of seeing beyond the difficulties of the text and moving into, through, and beyond the difficulties of the context is worth every effort that it takes to preach good news. It is the engagement of the divine call in the life and work of the preacher. It is not an exercise for the fainthearted, but its value is priceless and of inestimable worth to the people of God, whether or not they acknowledge it or even know it. The preacher digs deep not only into the recesses of history but also into the recesses of his or her heart to see the goodness of God that is present and that becomes visible beneath the scales of life's uncertainties and the vagaries of sin that infect human endeavors.

The tools described in chapter 1 offer a helpful guide for preaching good news from difficult texts, but they are, as stated, guidelines. They do not hold the answer to the location of the good news. The analysis of the congregation and the interpretation of the text may offer critical information for preaching, but even then there is no guarantee that the sermon will offer the transformative love of God that is essential to meeting the hearers' need to know God's grace in their lives. Ultimately that is the preacher's responsibility, and it is met only with the help of the Holy Spirit.

TEXT VERSUS CONTEXT

Preaching occurs at the intersection of text and context. Eunjoo Kim names "context as the locus of God's revelation."[1] It is the place where the history of God's self-revelation to the people of God meets the active presence of God in the lives of the waiting congregation. It is neither fully located in time or in a physical location, but it is realized in the ever-changing, ever-revealing presence of God in the midst of human endeavor. As Kim points out, the context of preaching is compounded by the global nature of the world in which we live and requires preachers "to take into account the growing nature of interconnectedness . . . (and) they should be familiar with a transcontextual approach that integrates particularity with global realities."[2] For the preacher who dares to approach the difficulties posed by text and context or text in context in the global nature of our world and the constancy of its ever-changing, ever-shrinking size and culture, the challenge may seem daunting in its magnitude. However, there are two constants that guide and provide direction in developing good news sermons in the face of difficult situations.

The first is that the grace of God is constant and unchanging. Regardless of the challenge the text offers, the reality of God's grace for humanity is absolute and dependable. The second constant in the midst of a world of change is humanity's need for God's grace. It is the impetus that moves the preacher to engage the biblical texts (or it should be), and it is the motivation that brings the members of the body of Christ to seek a fresh supply of God's grace from the words of the preacher. The crises of human injustice, oppression, and violence are rampant in the world, and the need to hear of God's unparalleled love incarnated in the life, death, and resurrection of Jesus Christ is as new in this time as it was in the time when the church came into being. The love of God for humanity, begun in creation, is as fresh and full as it was during both the exodus and the exile of the children of Israel, and it deserves recognition and celebration at this time in history when the exodus of refugees and newly exiled peoples still struggle to find their promised land among societies that bring laws to bear that not only deny them a place of rest but their very humanity.

Within the global context of life in the present, the biblical text must be made genuinely available to the people of God so that repentance and renewal can be sought as readily as refreshment and new life. The preacher's task calls for an immersion by faith into the biblical stories, however clouded or difficult, and through divinely inspired interpretation of both text and context, a bringing to light the grace of God that never fails to overcome human sin. Before beginning any activity that is intended to produce the finished product of a sermon, the would-be preacher who dares to address the people in the name of God wisely investigates the substance, norms, and exigencies of their particular culture; their ways of life; the doctrines that shape their faith and Christian beliefs; their worldviews; and their notions of God and justice as key elements of the Christian ethos, practices, and inherent beliefs that have contributed to their formation. The issues of epistemology, ecclesiology, even philosophy and psychology—not to mention theology, Christology, pneumatology, creation, and eschatology—all have significance for the people's ability to hear the message, to receive good news, and to advance their Christian discipleship.

Difficult texts require a deep level of interpretation so that the words are not misread or misapplied to the preaching context. In addition, given the limitations inherent in the English language, it may be important to review the meaning of the text in earlier languages in order to understand the nuances and shades of meaning that allow the meaning of the scripture text to come to light but that are not represented in the common vernacular. The guidelines provided for interpreting both text and context are intended to help the preacher not only unearth the hidden meanings of the text, but also to connect them with the situation of the intended hearers of the sermon and through it to offer a divine response to human dilemmas of faith and practice.

The idea of developing a good news statement is one that I recommend strongly as a discipline for ensuring that the sermon offers real and transformative good news. The students in my classes generally find this a difficult exercise, because the statement requires an active verb that shows God's action in a way that directly impacts the hearers. Even when the text itself does not qualify as difficult, it does not always offer an easy response to the idea of God's active participation in human life. There is great temptation to make the text say what the preacher considers it needs to say in order to represent the reality of the divine presence transforming human life for the better.

Almost certainly when there is difficulty in discerning the working of God's grace to bring about transformation, finding good news for preaching in difficult texts and challenging contexts requires the preacher to delve deeply into the texts of scripture to unearth the truths that are often hidden in the shadows of history and to decipher their meaning for the age and time. It means learning new languages that can speak to hearts and minds of multiple generations and belief systems and situations. It means unmasking oppression and injustice in the text and context and replacing it with a holy and living love from God that reaches out to every neighbor and every community with tentacles of grace that can cover all sin. To go beyond the obvious trouble and grace in each text means to plumb the depths and scale the heights of God's amazing love for the joy of celebrating that love with the people of God.

A SAVING GRACE

The relationship between God and humanity brings into stark reality the destructive force of human sin and the restorative grace of God that overcomes that sin, regardless of how heinous it may be. The grace of God that prevails is the evidence of the covenantal love of God that has continually offered redemption to a people who constantly and consistently reject the guiding hand of God on their lives. Preaching the good news of the whole Bible provides an opportunity to present the evidence of God's constancy in loving and forgiving sinful humanity. It enables the preacher to be evidence of that same grace as she or he struggles against her or his own inadequacies to shine the light of Immanuel found in even the difficult texts of scripture into the midst of the people of God.

The context of preaching is always the gathered community under the Lordship of Jesus Christ. Preaching is a doxological response of the worshiping community, led by the preacher, but experienced by the entire congregation. Scripture assures us that Christ is always in the midst of fallen humanity, picking us up and restoring us individually and shaping us as the beloved community. By the power of divine love, we are brought into right relationship with God and with one another. The good news sermon that is wrested from difficult texts and contexts of preaching offers a place where the revelation of the saving grace of God can be experienced by the gathered community. The preacher who succeeds in claiming good news from the clouds of trouble that envelops the difficult, troublesome, or excessively dense Bible texts does so by the same grace that the sermon offers, and that preacher experiences the same joy of knowing God's active presence as does the congregation, to whom God's presence is revealed through the sermon.

More than that, retrieving the evidence and depositing it in the midst of the congregation, who are themselves caught in the grip of doubt, despair, violence, injustice, or any of the issues of trouble that are part and parcel of life, offers its own reward to the preacher. That reward is the knowledge that once again God's love has been revealed and made real to the people of God. It is the acknowledgement of the power of the Holy Spirit operating in the lives of preacher and people to call them to bask in the glow of the everlasting light of God that enables them to shine with refracted light from the divine source and be themselves lights for God, empowered by the saving grace of God. In other words, the good news sermon developed against the background of troublesome texts and contexts is proof positive that we have been saved by grace once again. And undeserved or even unexpected, the people of God have received again the inestimable gift of God: saving grace for the people of God. And for that we say, thanks be to God.

APPENDIX A

Methodology for Developing Good News Sermons from Difficult Texts

•   •   •

The four steps outlined are guidelines for engaging the process of developing the sermon.

1. Analysis of the Preaching Context

This first task enables the preacher to understand the people and the situation to which the text will be preached. It is essential in determining what aspect of the biblical text preached in the sermon will connect to the context of the congregation.

2. Interpretation of the Biblical Text

The exegesis of the text may involve several modes of biblical interpretation. This task of listening to the text and allowing it to speak in its own contexts helps the preacher to avoid misrepresenting the contents and meaning of the text.

3. Creation of a Good News Statement and a Discipleship Message

Creating a good news statement offers a helpful exercise to verify that the good news represents the transformative action of God, present in human lives. The format of the good news statement has God as the subject of the action and human beings as the recipients of God's action: for example, *God strengthen the weak.*

The discipleship message invites the recipients of the good news to live fully into their identity as Christians. It is a directive statement that encourages the hearers to live actively into their discipleship: for example, *Go forward trusting in God to sustain you.*

4. Development of the Sermon

The sermon may be expository and focus almost myopically on a specific text, or topical and use a specific and difficult text as foundational scripture for the particular focus of a topical sermon.

APPENDIX B

Guidelines for Analysis of the Context

•   •   •

The following questions and directives should provide sufficient material for understanding the context in which the sermon will be preached.

Meeting the Congregation

- What are the demographics of your congregation? Age ranges, generations, family groups?
- Is there a situation in the life of the congregation for which the text has relevance?
- Are there current issues in the life of the congregation that will be brought to mind upon their hearing the text?
- What is the likely response of the congregation to the text (before the sermon is preached)?
- What in hearing the text may offend or challenge, instruct or affirm the hearers?
- What would be the immediate reaction or response to the text by the congregation?
- How does this text achieve significance for the present congregation?

- What is the social, cultural, theological, and doctrinal situation of the congregation?
- Based on history or their current situation, what might the congregation's expectation be of good news or a discipleship message from this text?

Culture and Community

- Consider the location of the congregation. Is it rural, urban, suburban?
- Does the location have significance for the people's ability to receive the message?
- Are there broader social and economic issues that need to be addressed?
- Is there a situation in the society or the world for which this text or topic has relevance at this time?
- Is the issue of justice a relevant and active element of the life of the community?

Preaching Context

- Is this sermon for a regular Sunday worship service or a special event?
- Does the liturgical season have relevance for the preaching context?
- Are there societal or world events that would influence the preaching event and require specific attention in the sermon?
- Why is the preaching of this text important or significant for the congregation at this time?
- Does the presentation of this text relate to a particular situation?

APPENDIX C

Guidelines for Homiletical Exegesis for Good News Preaching

• • •

The following suggestions and questions are not all-inclusive for biblical interpretation but are appropriate to providing exegetical material necessary for engaging the biblical text for preaching.

1. Meeting the text:

- Approach the text with expectation.
- Read through the text aloud several times, each time with a different emphasis.
- Jot down initial impressions, questions, and initial sermon ideas.

2. Locate the text historically:

- What is the historical setting and how much of it does your sermon require?
- Who was the author of the text?
- Where was the text written?
- When was the text written?
- What was the situation for which the text was written?
- Why was the text written?

3. Engage your senses and emotions in the reading of the text:

- What do you see, hear, smell, taste, and touch as you read the text?

- What emotions do you experience as you read the text?

- Having immersed yourself in the historical event, how do you think it felt to be in that situation?

- How much of the feeling of the first hearers would you like to relay to your congregation?

4. Identify the key words in the text:

- Which words have history that bears examination?

- Which words have greatest (and least) relevance for the present reality?

- Which words may require research in biblical languages?

5. Identify the form of the text:

- Is the form of the text narrative/nonnarrative, saga, myth, legend, historical narrative, scholastic, dialogue, or parable?

- Does the form influence the reading of the text or offer a model for the sermon?

6. Placement of the selected text within the corpus:

- What is the level of authorship—historical event, oral tradition, or redactor?

- Is there special significance to its placement?

- How is this passage used in the context of the corpus?

7. The context of the text:

- What are the social, religious, cultural, or other realities that confront or are confronted by the text in its original setting?

- How did it function in and affect the lives of those who heard it first?

- Are there parallels to be made with the current situation of the congregation?

APPENDIX D

*Guidelines for Developing the Good News Statement
and the Message Statement*

• • •

GOOD NEWS STATEMENT

This is a declarative statement that speaks of divine action doing the work of transformation in human lives. The structure is:

subject = God/Christ/Holy Spirit
verb = transformative action of God
object = human recipients of God's action

For example: *God strengthens the weak.*

MESSAGE STATEMENT

Proceeding from the good news, this is a directive that encourages the hearers in their Christian discipleship. Using the preceding example: Because the weak are made strong by God's action, they can live appropriately as Christians.

Thus an appropriate message statement would be: *Go forward, trusting in God to sustain you.*

NOTES

• • •

Preface

1. Gennifer Benjamin Brooks, *Good News Preaching: Offering the Gospel in Every Sermon* (Cleveland: Pilgrim Press, 2009). The thesis of this book is that every sermon must be intentional and specific in offering transformative good news.

2. Brooks, *Good News Preaching*, 8. Chapter 1 provides a process for identifying and defining the good news for preaching from a biblical text.

3. Paul Scott Wilson, *The Four Pages of the Sermon: A Guide to Biblical Preaching* (Nashville: Abingdon Press, 1999). Wilson's sermonic structure names two pages of human trouble and two pages of divine grace that responds to the human trouble. The trouble and grace present in the text are the models that find a parallel in the present context of the world.

4. This twelve-volume set, an update of an earlier set of commentaries, represents significant biblical scholarship in both Testaments provided by many respected scholars in the field of biblical studies.

5. See Catherine Gunsalus Gonzales, *Difficult Texts: The Great Texts— a Preaching Commentary* (Nashville: Abingdon Press, 2005). The author focuses on selected topics and uses several texts to interpret each topic for preaching that brings to light the difficulty in preaching the topic.

Chapter 1

1. Brooks, *Good News Preaching*, 66.

2. Ibid.

3. Gonzalez, *Difficult Texts*, 1.

4. Ibid.

5. Brooks, *Good News Preaching*, 55.

6. Ibid., xiii.

7. Wilson, *Four Pages of the Sermon*, 12.

8. Ibid., 13.

9. Ibid., 11–12. Wilson posits that "movies address the need for creative imagination" as requisite for preaching to twenty-first century congregations."

10. Wilson, *Four Pages of the Sermon*, 10–12.

11. Brooks, *Good News Preaching*, 4. Although stated differently in that text, the substance of the definition is the same.

12. Frank Thomas, *They Like to Never Quit Praisin' God: The Role of Celebration in Preaching* (Cleveland: United Church Press, 1997), 3. Thomas offers a celebrative style commonly used in the African American church to describe the congregational response to divine grace operating in the individual and corporate lives of the community. He says: "African American preaching is about helping people experience the assurance of grace that is the gospel" of Jesus Christ.

13. Appendix A provides an annotated outline of this methodological process, which is described in detail in this chapter.

14. Nancy T. Ammerman, Jackson W. Canal, Carl S. Dudley, and William McKinney, eds, *Studying Congregations: A New Handbook* (Nashville: Abingdon Press, 1998). This handbook invites the readers "to engage in a systematic look at congregational life."

15. Jackson W. Carroll, Carl S. Dudley, and William McKinney, eds., *Handbook for Congregation Studies* (Nashville; Abingdon Press, 1986). The authors articulate a framework for understanding congregations in their identity as the vessel for God's work on earth.

16. Brooks, *Good News Preaching*, 28.

17. Ibid., 7.

18. See Ronald J. Allen, ed., *Patterns of Preaching: A Sermon Sampler* (St. Louis: Chalice Press, 1998), for an explanation and sample of thirty-four different styles of sermons.

Chapter 2

1. Wikipedia: The Free Encyclopedia reports that the Gottfried Leibniz's *Theodicy Essays on the Goodness of God, the Freedom of Man, and the Origin of Evil*, English transl. (Peru, IL: Open Court, 1985), was written in part to show that the evil in the world does not conflict with the goodness of God.

2. Theodore Hiebert, "Excursus: The Moral Dilemma of the Sacrifice of Isaac," in *The New Interpreter's Study Bible* (Nashville: Abingdon Press, 2003), 43.

3. Brooks, *Good News Preaching*, 15.

4. Elizabeth Achtemeier, *Preaching Hard Texts of the Old Testament* (Peabody, MA.: Hendrickson, 1998), 20.

5. Ibid.

6. Ibid., 18–23.

7. Lisa Davison, "Commentary on Job," in *The New Interpreter's Study Bible* (Nashville: Abingdon Press, 2003), 703.

8. Carol A. Newsom, expositor, *The Book of Job*, vol. 4 in *The New Interpreter's Bible: A Commentary in Twelve Volumes* (Nashville: Abingdon Press, 1996), 319.

Chapter 3

1. Frank M. Yamada, *Configurations of Rape in the Hebrew Bible: A Literary Analysis of Three Rape Narratives* (New York: Peter Lang, 2008), 36.

2. Statistics were taken from the Rape Abuse and Incest National Network and the Bureau of Justice websites.

3. Yamada, *Configurations of Rape*, 39–40.

4. See the Domestic Violence Resource Center website for more information on domestic violence.

5. Yamada, *Configurations of Rape*, 128.

6. *Merriam Webster's Collegiate Dictionary*, 10th ed. (Springfield, Mass.: 1993), 930.

7. R. Allen Culpepper, *Luke–John*, vol. 9 in *The Interpreter's Bible: A Commentary in Twelve Volumes* (Nashville: Abingdon Press, 2002), 300.

Chapter 4

1. Robert W. Wall, *The Acts of the Apostles*, vol. 10 in *The New Interpreter's Bible: A Commentary in Twelve Volumes* (Nashville: Abingdon Press, 2002), 53.

2. Ibid., 54.

3. Ibid.

4. Ibid., 53–54.

5. The complete sermon is available in Gennifer Benjamin Brooks, *Black United Methodists Preach!* (Nashville: Abingdon Press, 2012). The sermon, "What God Tells Us: Imitate!" was preached by Rev. Leo W. Curry at Fordham United Methodist Church, Bronx, New York, February 16, 2011.

6. Obery M. Hendricks Jr., *The Politics of Jesus: Rediscovering the True Revolutionary Nature of Jesus' Teachings and How They Have Been Corrupted* (New York: Doubleday, 2006), 132–144.

7. Ibid., 133.

8. Ibid., 144.

Chapter 5

1. The term "social holiness" was John Wesley's descriptor for the holy life of a congregation.

2. United Methodist bishop Reuben P. Job has offered a modern reading of Wesley's rules that have been translated as: "Do no harm. Do good. Stay in love with God." See Job's *Three Simple Rules: A Wesleyan Way of Living* (Nashville: Abingdon Press, 2007) for his interpretation.

3. Robin R. Meyers, *Saving Jesus: How to Stop Worshipping Christ and Start Following Jesus* (New York: Harper One, 2009), 145.

4. N. T. Wright, expositor, "The Letter to the Romans," in vol. 10 of *The New Interpreter's Bible: A Commentary in Twelve Volumes* (Nashville: Abingdon Press, 2002), 704.

5. John Wesley developed a process that he called The Way of Salvation and preached many sermons on the various steps along the way. His sermon "Christian Perfection" (1741), in *The Works of John Wesley*, vol 2 (Nashville: Abingdon Press, 1987), expounded on the steps and the requirements of attaining perfection in life.

6. N. T. Wright, *Evil and the Justice of God* (Downers Grove, Ill.: InterVarsity Press, 2006), 120.

7. See "A Service of Word and Table IV," in *The United Methodist Hymnal* (Nashville, Tennessee: Abingdon Press, 1989), 26.

8. N. T. Wright, *What Saint Paul Really Said: Was Paul of Tarsus the Real Founder of Christianity?* (Grand Rapids: Eerdmans, 1977), 143.

9. Wall, *Acts,* xxx.

10. Ibid.

11. Cheryl B. Anderson, *Ancient Laws & Contemporary Controversies: The Need for Inclusive Biblical Interpretation* (Oxford, U.K.: Oxford University Press, 2009), 96.

Chapter 6

1. Eunjoo Mary Kim, *Preaching in an Age of Globalization* (Louisville: Westminster John Knox Press, 2010), 20.

2. Ibid., 20–21.

BIBLIOGRAPHY

• • •

Achtemeier , Elizabeth. *Preaching Hard Texts of the Old Testament.* Peabody, Mass.: Hendrickson, 1998.

Allen, O. Wesley. *The Homiletic of ALL Believers: A Conversational Approach.* Louisville: Westminster John Knox Press, 2005.

Allen, Ronald J. *Preaching: An Essential Guide.* Nashville: Abingdon Press, 2002.

————. ed. *Patterns of Preaching: A Sermon Sampler.* St. Louis: Chalice Press, 1998.

Ammerman, Nancy T., Jackson W. Carroll, Carl S. Dudley, and William McKinney, eds. *Studying Congregations: A New Handbook.* Nashville: Abingdon Press, 1998.

Anderson, Cheryl B. *Ancient Laws & Contemporary Controversies: The Need for Inclusive Biblical Interpretation.* Oxford, UK: Oxford University Press, 2009.

————. *Women, Ideology and Violence: Critical Theory and the Construction of Gender in the Book of the Covenant and the Deuteronomic Law.* London: T&T Clark, 2004.

Bailey, Wilma Ann. *"You Shall Not Kill" or "You Shall Not Murder": The Assault on a Biblical Text.* Collegeville, MN: Liturgical Press, 2005.

Barth, Karl. *The Humanity of God.* Atlanta: John Knox Press, 1960.

Bartlett, David L. *Between the Bible and the Church: New Methods for Biblical Preaching.* Nashville: Abingdon Press, 1999.

Bohler, Carolyn Jane. *God the What? What Our Metaphors for God Reveal about Our Beliefs in God.* Woodstock, VT: Skylight Paths, 2008.

Bond, L. Susan. *Trouble with Jesus: Women, Christology and Preaching.* St. Louis: Chalice Press, 1999.

Brooks, Gennifer Benjamin. *Good News Preaching: Offering the Gospel in Every Sermon.* Cleveland: Pilgrim Press, 2009.

———. *Black United Methodist Preach!* Nashville: Abingdon Press, 2012.

Burghardt, Walter J., S.J. *Preaching the Just Word.* New Haven, CT: Yale University Press, 1996.

Buttrick, David. *Speaking Conflict: Stories of a Controversial Jesus.* Louisville: Westminster John Knox Press, 2007.

Carrol, John T. and James R. Carroll. *Preaching the Hard Sayings of Jesus.* Peabody, MA: Hendrickson, 1998.

Carroll, Jackson W., Carl S. Dudley, and William McKinney, eds. *Handbook for Congregational Studies.* Nashville: Abingdon Press, 1986.

Ebeling, Jennie R. *Women's Lives in Biblical Times.* New York: T&T Clark, 2010.

Gibson, Scott M., ed. *Preaching the Old Testament.* Grand Rapids: Baker Books, 2006.

Green, Joel B. *Seized by Truth: Reading the Bible as Scripture.* Nashville: Abingdon Press, 2007.

Gonzalez, Catherine Gunsalus. *Difficult Texts: The Great Texts—A Preaching Commentary.* Nashville: Abingdon Press, 2005.

Gonzalez, Justo, and Catherine G. Gonzalez. *The Liberating Pulpit.* Wipf and Stock, 2003.

Hendricks, Obery M. Jr. *The Politics of Jesus: Rediscovering the True Revolutionary Nature of Jesus' Teachings and How They Have Been Corrupted.* New York: Doubleday, 2006.

Hogan, Lucy Lind. *Graceful Speech: An Invitation to Preaching.* Louisville: Westminster John Knox Press, 2006.

Jeter, Joseph R., and Ronald J. Allen. *One Gospel, Many Ears: Preaching for Different Listeners in the Congregation.* St. Louis: Chalice Press, 2002.

Johnson, Graham. *Preaching to a Postmodern World: A Guide to Reaching Twenty-First Century Listeners.* Grand Rapids: Baker Books, 2001.

Kim, Eunjoo Mary. *Preaching in an Age of Globalization.* Louisville: Westminster John Knox Press, 2010.

Lapsley, Jacqueline E. *Whispering the Word: Hearing Women's Stories in the Old Testament.* Louisville: Westminster John Knox Press, 2005.

Lowry, Eugene. *The Sermon: Dancing on the Edge of Mystery.* Nashville: Abingdon Press, 1997.

Ludemann, Gerd. *The Unholy in Holy Scripture: The Dark Side of the Bible.* Louisville: Westminster John Knox Press, 1996, 2002.

Meyers, Robin, R. *Saving Jesus: How to Stop Worshipping Christ and Start Following Jesus.* New York: HarperOne, 2009.

The New Interpreter's Bible: A Commentary in Twelve Volumes. Nashville: Abingdon Press, 1996, 2002.

The New Interpreter's Study Bible. Nashville: Abingdon Press, 2003.

O'Day, Gail R. and Thomas G. Long, eds. *Listening to the Word.* Nashville: Abingdon Press, 1993.

Rice, Charles L. *The Embodied Word: Preaching as Art and Liturgy.* Minneapolis: Fortress Press, 1991.

Rose, Lucy Atkinson. *Sharing the Word: Preaching in the Roundtable Church.* Louisville: Westminster John Knox Press, 1997.

Sleeth, Ronald E. *God's Words and Our Words: Basic Homiletics.* Atlanta: John Knox Press, 1986.

Suchocki, Marjorie Hewitt. *The Whispered Word: A Theology of Preaching.* Saint Louis: Chalice Press, 1999.

Thomas, Frank A. *They Like to Never Quit Praisin' God: The Role of Celebration in Preaching.* Cleveland: United Church Press, 1997.

Tisdale, Nora Tubbs. *Preaching as Local Theology and Folk Art.* Minneapolis: Fortress Press, 1997.

Ward, Richard F. *Speaking of the Holy: The Art of Communication in Preaching.* St. Louis: Chalice Press, 2001.

Webb, Stephen H. *The Divine Voice: Christian Proclamation and the Theology of Sound.* Grand Rapids: Brazos Press, 2004.

West, Traci C. *Wounds of the Spirit: Black Women, Violence, and Resistance Ethics.* New York: New York University Press, 1999.

Wilson, Paul Scott. *The Four Pages of the Sermon: A Guide to Biblical Preaching.* Nashville: Abingdon Press, 1999.

Wisdom, Andrew Carl. *Preaching to a Multi-generational Assembly.* Collegeville, MN: Liturgical Press, 2004.

Wright, N. T. *Evil and the Justice of God.* Downers Grove, IL: InterVarsity Press, 2006.

————. *The Last Word: Beyond the Bible Wars to a New Understanding of the Authority of Scripture*. New York: HarperSanFrancisco, 2005.

————. *What Saint Paul Really Said: Was Paul of Tarsus the Real Founder of Christianity?* Grand Rapids: Eerdmans, 1977.

Yamada, Frank M. *Configurations of Rape in the Hebrew Bible: A Literary Analysis of Three Rape Narratives*. New York: Peter Lang, 2008.